About the Authors

HOWARD ZINN is professor emeritus at Boston University. He is the author of numerous books, including the classic *A People's History of the United States*.

Zinn has received the Lannan Foundation Literary Award for Nonfiction, and the Eugene V. Debs Award for his writing and political activism. In 2003 he was awarded the Prix des Amis du Monde Diplomatique.

Zinn grew up in Brooklyn. Before serving as an Air Force bombardier in World War II, he worked in the Brooklyn shipyards. Zinn was chair of the history department at Spelman College, where he was active in the civil rights movement. After taking a position at Boston University, he became a leader in the movement to end the war in Vietnam. Zinn continues to be active and now lectures widely on history, contemporary politics, and against war.

He lives with his wife, Roslyn, in Massachusetts.

DAVID BARSAMIAN, founder and director of the widely syndicated weekly show *Alternative Radio*, has authored several books of interviews with leading political thinkers, including Arundhati Roy, Howard Zinn, Tariq Ali, and Noam Chomsky. Barsamian is the recipient of the ACLU's Upton Sinclair Award for independent journalism. He lives in Boulder, Colorado.

Books by Howard Zinn

Voices of a People's History of the United States
(with Anthony Arnove)

*The People Speak: American Voices, Some Famous,
Some Little Known*

Artists in Times of War

Passionate Declarations: Essays on War and Justice

*You Can't Be Neutral on a Moving Train:
A Personal History of Our Times* (2nd ed.)

Terrorism and War (with Anthony Arnove)

Emma (a play)

A People's History of the United States: 1492–Present (updated ed.)

*Three Strikes: Miners, Musicians, Salesgirls, and the Fighting Spirit
of Labor's Last Century*
(with Dana Frank and Robin D. G. Kelley)

Howard Zinn on War

Howard Zinn on History

La otra historia de los Estados Unidos

Marx in Soho: A Play on History

The Future of History: Interviews with David Barsamian

The Zinn Reader: Writings on Disobedience and Democracy

Failure to Quit: Reflections of an Optimistic Historian (reprint ed.)

The Politics of History (2nd ed.)

Justice: Eyewitness Accounts (reprint ed.)

Postwar America: 1945–1971 (reprint ed.)

Disobedience and Democracy: Nine Fallacies of Law and Order (reprint ed.)

Vietnam: The Logic of Withdrawal (reprint ed.)

SNCC: The New Abolitionists (reprint ed.)

The Southern Mystique (reprint ed.)

LaGuardia in Congress

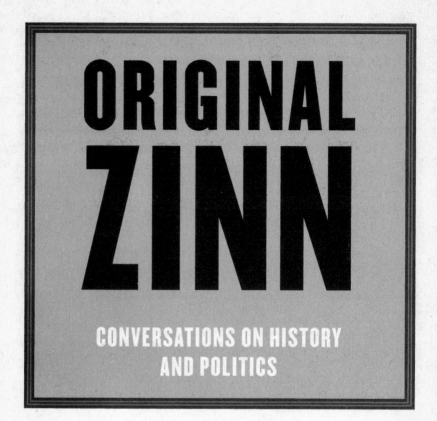

ORIGINAL ZINN

CONVERSATIONS ON HISTORY AND POLITICS

Howard Zinn
with David Barsamian

Foreword by Arundhati Roy

HARPER PERENNIAL

NEW YORK • LONDON • TORONTO • SYDNEY

HARPER ● PERENNIAL

HarperCollins books may be purchased for educational, business, or sales promotional use. For information please write: Special Markets Department, HarperCollins Publishers, 10 East 53rd Street, New York, NY 10022.

FIRST EDITION

Designed by Jamie Kerner-Scott

Library of Congress Cataloging-in-Publication Data

Zinn, Howard.
Original Zinn : conversations on history and politics / Howard Zinn with David Barsamian ; foreword by Arundhati Roy.— 1st ed.
    p. cm.
ISBN-10: 0-06-084425-6
ISBN-13: 978-0-06-084425-7
1. World politics—Twentieth century. 2. United States—Politics and government—Twentieth century. 3. History—Philosophy. 4. Ideology. 5. Zinn, Howard—Interviews. 6. Historians—United States—Interviews. I. Barsamian, David. II. Title.
    D445.Z55 2006
    973.072'02—dc22

                                    2005055107

06 07 08 09 10 ❖/RRD 10 9 8 7 6 5 4 3 2 1

CONTENTS

FOREWORD

Howard Zinn is a historian, a teacher who belongs to that most unusual tradition of academics—intellectually rigorous but unafraid of taking sides when it is right and just to take sides. Not for him that pusillanimous fancy footwork that masquerades these days as intellectual sophistication. The title of his lucid, engaging autobiography, *You Can't Be Neutral on a Moving Train*, is a clear giveaway of the kind of man he is.

In an age when the U.S. government's ruthless military interventions have begun to fuel a kind of crude anti-Americanism, Howard Zinn's work is doubly important. It shows us the rich tradition of resistance that has taken place in the heart of Empire. You need only read his books *A People's History of the United States*, *Voices of a People's History of the United States* (with Anthony Arnove), or the interviews here to understand this.

Zinn's work exemplifies an *approach* to history that is radical, regardless of its subject or geographical location. He tells us the untold story, the story of the world's poor, the world's workers, the world's homeless, the world's oppressed, the people who don't really qualify as real people in official histories. Howard Zinn painstakingly unearths the details that the powerful seek to airbrush away. He brings official secrets and forgotten histories into the light and, in doing so, changes the official narrative that the powerful have constructed for us. He strips the grinning mask off the myth of the benign U.S. Empire.

Not to read Howard Zinn is to do a disservice to yourself.

—Arundhati Roy

ORIGINAL
ZINN

1

CAN THE SYSTEM BE FIXED?

KGNU, Boulder, Colorado
August 8, 2002

I want to start with something from F. Scott Fitzgerald's Great Gatsby, *a novel about the Roaring Twenties and the excesses that character-ized that period just before the Great Depression. Fitzgerald wrote, "They were careless people. . . . they smashed up things and creatures and then retreated back into their money or their vast carelessness, or whatever it was that kept them together, and let other people clean up the mess they had made."*

It's interesting that you should quote Fitzgerald. The twenties have much in common with what we are seeing today. Then there were governments in power that insisted on distributing the wealth of the country in such a way that the rich got richer and the poor were stuck where they were or got even poorer. Wild speculation took place. Vast fortunes were made, while people in poor areas of cities were struggling to pay the rent and put food on the table. It was capitalism run amok. Interestingly, Pope John Paul II, in an inter-view in an Italian newspaper, talked about "savage, unbridled capi-talism." That's what we saw in the twenties and that's what we are seeing today. Except that today it is even more unbridled, more savage.

And it is running amok on a global scale. It is causing havoc in various countries. Here in the United States many people are in desperate circumstances without medical care, adequate housing, and education.

Why is it that crime in the streets has historically attracted much more attention than what Ralph Nader calls crime in the suites, white-collar crime?

There are several reasons. The people who define crime are connected to those in the suites. They are the ones who say what it is. If somebody holds up a store or robs someone on the street, of course those are crimes. If somebody robs consumers of millions of dollars or robs workers of their lives because of unsafe work conditions, that's not crime. That's business. The media constantly focus on mayhem being done by ordinary people. But what is being done by the corporate giants usually doesn't get into the media until it explodes in a wave of scandals as we have now. There are other reasons for the emphasis on street crime over corporate crime. Street crime is overt, whereas the corporate variety is secret. It is therefore important to have some individuals point out what is being done in secret. At the turn of the century, they were called muckrakers. People like Lincoln Steffens and Ida Tarbell exposing the doings of the Standard Oil Company. In the twenties, there was Fiorello LaGuardia, a congressman from East Harlem, who criticized the rich because the poor in his district were struggling to make ends meet. And today we have our muckrakers. There's Jim Hightower and Barbara Ehrenreich. Ralph Nader has long fought corporate crime. We need to seek out the information that the muckrakers of our time are putting out so that they we aren't completely ignorant of what is going on.

To provide more historical context, how would you compare the current era to that of the robber barons in the late nineteenth century? And explain who they were.

There is a remarkable book by Matthew Josephson entitled *The Robber Barons.* They were the great corporate executives and moguls of the late nineteenth century, such as the Vanderbilts, Hills, and Harrimans who controlled the railroads; the Carnegies and Mellons who controlled steel and aluminum; the J. P. Morgans who worked out deals by merging companies and making huge profits thereby. They were the people who manipulated the money market. The robber barons owned the factories where workers toiled for fourteen hours a day. They were the counterparts of what we have seen in the twentieth and now the twenty-first centuries: the CEOs making enormous sums of money and laying off their workers without taking care of their health insurance; leaving the workers in the lurch when they are fifty or sixty years old, after having lost their retirement benefits. These are the robber barons of today.

One of the fastest-growing groups entering the job market are people in the fifty-five- to seventy-year-old age bracket who have to go back to work to support themselves.

What is interesting to me is how the word *security* is bandied about by the government. In the name of security, they fingerprint and keep tabs on people and pick them up in the middle of the night, especially noncitizens and even some who are citizens. A large part of our national wealth is being given to the military budget. And it is all being done in the name of security. While the security of people in their daily lives is being taken away from them. Real security is the security people need when they get to the age when they want to stop working. Or the security that all people need to be able to deal with their medical problems without incurring huge bills that they can't pay. The security of having work when you are able to work. And there are things to be done in the country. The security that children need to grow up in healthy environments. That kind of security is simply put aside while the militarization of the country goes on.

Is the current crisis of capitalism a systemic one?

It is systemic in the sense that it is not just an aberration that will pass if and when a few corporate crooks go to prison. The stock market may go up again. But the fundamental sickness of the system remains. By that I mean that even when the stock market is up and even when the worst excesses of the corporate system have been slightly corrected, fundamental problems remain. And those are the maldistribution of wealth, with one percent of the country owning 40 percent of the wealth; huge salaries at the top; people struggling below; homeless people; many Americans living in inadequate housing, unable to pay the rent.

It is systemic because there is something fundamentally flawed in the economic system. And I believe what is fundamental about the capitalist system, and is a systemic problem, is that profit is the driving force that decides what is done in society. That is basic. That profit motive means that homes will not be built for low-income people because there is no money to be made that way. Teachers' salaries will not be doubled, as they should be. The rivers, lakes, and oceans will not be cleaned up because there is no profit in it. We are not going to curtail the emissions from cars that are polluting the atmosphere and destroying the environment for ourselves and our children because that will cut into the profits of the automobile manufacturers. Nuclear weapons are made and Sikorsky helicopters are made because they are profitable. The incentive of profit, which people who want to glorify our system describe as a wonderful thing, may lead to enormous production so that the gross national product rises and rises. But if you look at what that gross national product consists of, it is very gross. It consists of things that do not solve the day-to-day needs of ordinary citizens. It consists of machines of war and luxuries for the rich. Our leaders talk happily about exporting the free market system and private enterprise to other countries so that they will prosper. But more and more countries are suffering not only because of our own multinational corporations but also because of the policies of the International Monetary Fund and the World Bank. So it is not only systemic for the United States, but also—since the United States is so dominant economically—systemic for the world at large.

The Italian writer and political thinker Antonio Gramsci died in 1937. He was a resistor to fascism. His health was broken by years in Mussolini's prisons. He wrote of the crisis then, "the old is dying and the new cannot be born. In this interregnum a great variety of morbid symptoms appear." Do you see the current domestic crisis and the broader international one demonstrating the kind of morbid symptoms that Gramsci referred to?

I am afraid so. When he talks about the old dying and the new not yet born and the morbid symptoms, that's a very gloomy picture. I'd like to think that, although the new has not yet been born and the old system has not yet died, the old system is beginning to reveal what is wrong with it in a way that will cause the new to emerge as more and more people rebel against the old. Supposedly powerless people have amazing power. There are women activists in Nigeria who shut down the Chevron Texaco operation. Poor people in Peru protesting the impact on them of the so-called free market system. Banana workers in Ecuador going on strike, evoking in a way what García Márquez wrote about in *One Hundred Years of Solitude*. In Poland there are signs of recognition that the lovely capitalist system that was promised for them has turned out to be disastrous. In short, Gramsci was accurately describing what he saw. But I'd like to look at it more dynamically. While a new way of life has not yet emerged, there are people all over the world who are beginning to understand that something fundamental is wrong and that something must be done. You might say that there are seeds of the rebellion against the old and the first signs of the emergence of something new.

Certainly since the Seattle protests in late 1999, there is a growing awareness of linking U.S. foreign policy with the economic and environmental well-being of the planet. The World Social Forum in Pôrto Alegre, Brazil, has drawn tens of thousands of social activists from all over. There are lots of movements out there.

Seattle was the beginning of a whole series of protests. It's interesting to me that when the World Economic Forum met earlier this year at the Waldorf=Astoria in New York, there were protestors not only outside but inside as well. They expressed their indignation at U.S. domination of economies and politics around the world. When you see dissent at the very top, inside the World Economic Forum, they are in part reflecting their recognition that there are people outside protesting. That number of people protesting may grow and grow. But they are also reflecting that people in their own countries— whether in Africa, Latin America, or Europe—are beginning to resent what the United States is doing in trying to create a new imperium in which the United States runs everything.

We began with F. Scott Fitzgerald. Let's continue with another novelist, Joseph Conrad. His Heart of Darkness *was published in 1902. He was aware of the Belgian atrocities in the Congo, one of the great crimes in history. Conrad wrote, "They were conquerors, and for that you only want brute force. . . . They grabbed what they could get for the sake of what was to be got. It was robbery with violence, aggravated murder on a great scale, and men going at it blind. . . . The conquest of the earth, which mostly means the taking it away from those who have a different complexion or slightly flatter noses than ourselves, is not a pretty thing when you look into it too much."*

Conrad through his literary writings was telling us the same thing that other people were telling us about the ugly and violent process by which Western nations conquered parts of the earth. It made me think of Barbara Kingsolver's beautifully written novel *The Poisonwood Bible* in which she writes about the Congo in our time. It also made me think of Adam Hochschild's *King Leopold's Ghost*, a historical study of what the Belgians did in the Congo. But that is something that has happened throughout Africa and other parts of the world in the nineteenth and into the twentieth century and continues into the present. Look at American policy in Latin America. What could be uglier or more violent than what the United States has done for over a century in Latin America? From the early dispatch of marines to Haiti and the Dominican Republic, and the taking over of Panama, and the domination of Cuba. And more recently the establishment of dictatorships in Guatemala and elsewhere in Latin America. And the deaths of hundreds of thousands of people as the result of what can only be described as American imperialism. It is a counterpart of what Conrad described in Africa. It may be an imperialism more concealed than the Belgian variety. That is to say, it is more surrounded in the rhetoric of kindly imperialism, sort of like what the British used in India. Lines like, "We are helping these people. We are doing things for them, etc." But in the end people suffered and died. In the case of the United States, the government has intervened on behalf of the interests of the oil companies, the sugar industry, the banks, and the railroads. The economic motive driving U.S. policy in Latin America is probably more stark and clear than anywhere else except perhaps for the control of oil in the Middle East. When the United States put Pinochet in power in Chile, that happened as the direct result of the influence of ITT and Anaconda Copper in overthrowing the democratically elected government of Salvador Allende. In Guatemala, Jacobo Arbenz, the head of another democratically elected government, was overthrown as the direct result of the connection between the United Fruit Company and the Eisenhower administration. So what Conrad writes about is still going on today.

Traditionally the term American imperialism *could not be mentioned in polite discourse, history books, or the media. That seems to be changing. There's a new book by Max Boot, taking its cue from Kipling's* White Man's Burden *entitled* The Savage Wars of Peace. *Another is a July 28* New York Times Magazine *cover story by Michael Ignatieff, "How to Keep Afghanistan from Falling Apart:*

The Case for a Committed American Imperialism." He is the Carr Professor of Human Rights Policy and Director of the Carr Center at the Kennedy School of Government at Harvard. He writes, "America's entire war on terror is an exercise in imperialism." Then he adds, "Imperialism used to be the white man's burden. This gave it a bad reputation. But imperialism doesn't stop being necessary just because it becomes politically incorrect."

It is ironic that Ignatieff should be Professor of Human Rights Policy. It does not seem to me that imperialism, certainly not American imperialism, has anything to do with the advancement of human rights. It is rather the opposite. His statement on the war on terrorism as an exercise in imperialism is accurate. The war is using terrorism as an excuse to advance American military and economic power to other parts of the world where they had not yet reached. When he says it is necessary, who is it necessary for? He is trying to suggest that imperialism now is a good thing. He says, imperialism had a bad reputation. Does it now have a good one? Can we point to wonderful things that have happened to countries under U.S. control and influence? Can we point to wonderful things that happened in Indonesia when the United States supported Suharto and his war against the people of East Timor, leaving several hundreds of thousands dead? Imperialism is as ugly and brutal as it always was. But it seems to be becoming important for its intellectual defenders to come forth in the pages of the *New York Times Magazine* and elsewhere and try to put a good face on what still is Kipling's "savage wars of peace."

One of the foot soldiers of imperialism was Major General Smedley Butler of the U.S. Marine Corps. He was a highly decorated officer, twice winning the Congressional Medal of Honor. This is from

Maverick Marine, a book by Hans Schmidt. Butler said, "I've spent thirty-three years . . . most of my time being a high-class muscle man for Big Business, for Wall Street and the bankers. In short, I was a racketeer for Capitalism . . . I helped purify Nicaragua. I helped make Mexico . . . safe for American oil interests. I helped in the rape of half a dozen Central American Republics for the benefit of Wall Street. . . . I was rewarded with honors, medals, promotions. . . . I might have given Al Capone a few hints. The best he could do was to operate a racket in three city districts. The Marines operated on three continents."

Smedley Butler is one of those great whistleblowers of history. People who come out of the establishment and turn around and expose what it has done. And they do it with authority because they participated in what was done. What he is describing is something that should be remembered when people read Michael Ignatieff. What is missing in the statements in support of the new imperialism by people like Ignatieff and others writing in the *New Republic* and elsewhere is any kind of understanding of the history of U.S. foreign policy. Their assumption is that the United States is going to send its troops around the world and that they are going to do good things and that their intentions are benign. This assumption totally collapses when you read the history of American marauding in the world, such as Smedley Butler describes. The history of U.S. expansionism is so long and odious that if you knew it you could not possibly talk about kindly motives. Only a lack of that history would allow people to believe that American power is going to be used for good. That history goes back to the extermination of Indian tribes, right on through the war with Mexico, and right up to today with the support for the armed forces of Colombia and the so-called war on terrorism.

Tariq Ali, the writer and political activist, comments that open decla-
rations of American imperialism may not be all that bad. He says,
"Now we know where to kneel."

[Laughter] I suppose you might say it's a good thing that they are
coming out of the closet. And saying, Yes, we are imperialists, but
we are nice imperialists. Because then all we need to do is to examine some history and we will see how nice our imperialism has
been. It is not just ancient history. Just look at recent years. It has
been the invasion of Panama, the Gulf War, the bombing of Yugo-
slavia. The United States calls Saddam Hussein an evil man. And
he is a terrible tyrant. But the United States has been behaving in
the most evil way in causing enormous privation and death in Iraq,
even beyond what Saddam Hussein has done to his own people.

You wrote an essay in the book Iraq Under Siege *and signed a peti-*
tion along with Noam Chomsky, Edward Said, Angela Davis, June
Jordan, and others saying that sanctions are weapons of mass destruc-
tion. Explain what you mean.

They are weapons of mass destruction because—and this is the testimony of Americans and others who have been in Iraq—the lack of
water, electricity, medicine, and basic necessities has resulted in the
deaths of several hundred thousand children. Several hundred
thousand children. Yes, I would consider sanctions to be weapons of
mass destruction. The whole issue of weapons of mass destruction
is so interesting because it is constantly brought forth as the reason
both for the sanctions and for the possible invasion of Iraq. The
country in the world that by far possesses the greatest number of
weapons of mass destruction is the United States of America. And
the United States talks about Saddam Hussein possibly, possibly,

acquiring one nuclear weapon; the United States has thousands of nuclear weapons. The United States says, but he has used his weapons. That's true. He gassed the Kurds in 1988, but the United States did not disapprove at that time. The United States has used its weapons of mass destruction from Hiroshima and Nagasaki on through Vietnam and the Gulf War, resulting in a far, far greater toll of human life than taken by any other country in the world. It is remarkably hypocritical of the United States to talk about weapons of mass destruction.

Senator Joseph Biden, a liberal democrat and chair of the Senate Foreign Relations Committee held hearings on Iraq in late July and early August. The usual suspects testified, such as Reagan Defense Secretary Caspar Weinberger and Clinton National Security Advisor Samuel Berger. What was noteworthy was the absence of critical voices like Kathy Kelly of the Chicago-based Voices in the Wilderness; Scott Ritter, the outspoken ex-marine and former weapons inspector in Iraq; Hans von Sponeck and Denis Halliday, two Assistant Secretary Generals of the UN who were in charge of the Oil for Food program in Iraq, both of whom resigned in protest over the devastation caused by the sanctions.

Congress has a long history of subservience when it comes to presidential plans for war. If you look at history, when the president has decided on war, Congress has never dissented. It has always rushed to support the president. I am not really surprised that Biden kept out of the hearings people who have been the closest observers of the situation in Iraq. Instead, he called on, as you said, the usual suspects. The people who will say what the administration wants them to say. It is not going to be Senate hearings that stop the war plans on Iraq. It is going to take resistance and protest by the American people, who will ask, Why should our young people die and why should Iraqis die for the ambition of oil companies and the political ambitions of American leaders? It will take protest from the grass roots rather than Senate hearings to turn American policy around.

Richard Falk in the August 19 issue of The Nation *has an article entitled "The Rush to War." It is about U.S. Iraq policy. He poses a series of questions at the end of his essay: "We must ask why the open American system is so closed in this instance? How can we explain this unsavory rush to judgment, when so many lives are at stake? What is now wrong with our system, with the vigilance of our citizenry, that such a course of action can be embarked upon without even evoking criticism in high places, much less mass opposition in the streets?" How would you respond to Falk?*

He should not be surprised. Citizens have never had an opportunity to express their dissent when the country goes to war. One of the reasons is that the media have always gone along with administration policy in preparing for and going to war. We have never really had an open system. We have had a system that has been largely closed. Citizens have had to create their own apertures, like independent newspapers and magazines, community radio stations, and *Alternative Radio*. Citizens have had to take advantage of the few apertures in the system in order to express their dissent. It is disturbing that we are not seeing mass revulsion against plans for war. But I believe the idea of going to war against Iraq is going to become more and more obviously wrong to more and more Americans.

How do you account for the dramatic difference in views on Iraq in Europe and other parts of the world compared to the United States? It seems we are living in our own bubble and having circular conversations, whereas the rest of world has different views.

The other countries do not see themselves as benefiting from American domination of oil and the Middle East. European nations have actually made arrangements with Iraq for oil. The United States does not like that. There is competition between Europe and the United States. There are conflicts of interests. The overseas media are not as willing to bow down before U.S. policy. And they are willing to educate their public in a way that our media are not willing to do.

2

THE BACKSEAT INTERVIEW, PART I

Albuquerque/Santa Fe, New Mexico
September 18, 2002

Studs Terkel says Americans suffer from a national Alzheimer's disease; we forget history.

Studs Terkel has a nice way of putting things, and of course he's right. We have a way of forgetting. We could put it another way. Our culture likes us to forget things, or the people in charge of our culture and the people in charge of the media and the people in charge of our education system would like us to forget certain things. Certainly the political leaders would like us to forget. And the result is, if the media and the cultural system and the political leaders all collaborate in trying to make us forget, yes, then we have a national case of Alzheimer's. And we couldn't have a better instance of it than when a war is pending. And it seems that in the history of the United States since the end of World War II, a war is almost always either on or pending. Now when you're in a war situation, or a near-war situation, that is exactly the time when the government would like the citizenry to forget history. Because if a citizenry remembered history, and then they listened to the leaders of the government get up before the microphones and say, "Well, it seems we need to go to war for this reason or that reason." We need to go to war to liberate South Korea, or we need to go to war to liberate South Vietnam, or all of Vietnam, or we need to go to war to end the drug problem in Panama, or we need to go to war because Grenada is an enormous threat to the security of the United States, or we need to go to war because Saddam Hussein invaded Kuwait. If people knew some history and they went back over all of those claims that the government made about why we need to go to war, they would know by this time that those claims were largely erroneous. Then people would be very skeptical if the government came to them at this point and said we need to go to war on Iraq because Saddam Hussein is a tyrant, or because Saddam Hussein has weapons of mass destruction, or because we are just a gentle giant in the world, and everything we do with our giantism is designed for the betterment of humanity. Well, if people knew history, they would scoff at that. They would laugh at that. They would get angry at that. And they would feel that the wealth and the younger generation of our country are about to be expended on the basis of a lie.

Rosa Parks is an interesting figure in American history. The conventional story about her is that she had a hard day at the office and was tired and decided not to sit in the back of the bus. But, in fact, the real Rosa Parks was someone quite different from that story.

The standard story omits important facts. The real story is not that she was an innocent who suddenly got tired, but she was an activist. She was a member of the NAACP. She had long been active against racial segregation in Montgomery, Alabama. She had gone to the Highlander Folk School, which was a kind of place that the establishment didn't like. Not only the southern establishment but also the northern establishment didn't like. It was a kind of oasis of interracial camaraderie in Tennessee, where people in the labor movement got together and people in the civil rights movement got together for conferences and workshops. And Martin Luther King was there. Andy Young was there. But the Highlander Folk School was looked upon as kind of outside the pale of respectability. It was too far to the left. And, in fact, when Martin Luther King went there, photographs were displayed in KKK and right-wing newspapers showing King there and saying he had attended a Communist establishment. Rosa Parks was a politically sophisticated and quite progressive person who got involved in the Montgomery bus situation quite deliberately and not by accident. And I think that that story is intended to be buried because when progress does take place, when remarkable events occur like the Montgomery Bus Boycott, the establishment doesn't want people to know that it comes as a result of long, persistent organization, patience, and education. Because that would suggest to the American people that that's the way change comes about. Not by accident but by deliberate organization.

The idea of an ideologically driven African American woman is threatening.

Yes, on a number of accounts. As you say, ideologically driven—that is, driven by ideas, driven by philosophy, driven by a point of view—and no, they don't want to suggest that the important actors in history have that kind of background. And certainly not a black woman. It goes against the orthodoxy of the establishment.

Another figure who has been compartmentalized is Martin Luther King Jr. Every January 15, on his birthday, the media air his "I have a dream" speech, given on the steps of the Lincoln Memorial in 1963. But there was another Martin Luther King that evolved in the last five years of his life. Particularly the one that gave a speech on Vietnam at Riverside Church in New York on April 4, 1967. Talk about that Martin Luther King.

King is sanitized and made to appear as sort of a nice man who "had a dream." But what they will never say is that King had a dream about socialism. That would shock people if you said King had a dream about socialism. But, in fact, King, in discussions with his staff in '66, '67, early '68, not long before he was killed, talked about the failure of the economic system, the failure of capitalism, and the connection between capitalism and militarism. And he said we need a kind of democratic socialism. That was, of course, a dream that is not going to be recorded by the major media. And it was even forgotten by a lot of people who want to go beyond the major media. King was quite radical in a number of ways. That Riverside Church speech was when he, for the first time publicly—he had been talking about it privately—denounced the U.S. government for its war in Vietnam. And said, in fact, that the United States was "the greatest purveyor of violence in the world today."

It was not easy for him to make that speech. That is, not easy in the sense that he was constantly in the position of having to deal with the other major civil rights leaders, such as Whitney Young of the Urban League and Roy Wilkins of the NAACP. These other leaders of the civil rights movement thought they should not speak out on Vietnam because it hurt their cause, because it would lose whatever capital they had built up with the establishment. But King was a person of principle and courage. He felt strongly about what we were doing in Vietnam, and he was determined to speak out. And he understood that militarism in the United States was tied up with the economic system, that it was built into American history. He was a pacifist. He was opposed to war in a very deep way. So, he was willing to break with the civil rights establishment and make this speech, which I think is a very important speech in telling black people in this country that, yes, their natural feelings of resentment against the United States could come out, that they didn't have to prove themselves, as very often black people thought they had to do, to be super patriots like other Americans; that they could come out and denounce American foreign policy. And I would put Martin Luther King's speech alongside Mohammad Ali's protest against the war, which cost him the title of heavyweight champion but which was one of the heroic acts of the Vietnam period.

But I want to say something else about Martin Luther King and his radicalism, which I think grew. It was there fundamentally with him as a young man as he studied Gandhi. He understood that there was something wrong with the American economic system, but I think his ideas on that crystallized more and more as the years went on. And by 1967–68 he was talking, in the way I just mentioned, to his staff. He had decided that now that certain gains had been won in the civil rights struggle—the Civil Rights Act of 1964 and the Voting Rights Act of 1965—the movement really did not know which way to turn at this point. And he saw that the way to turn was to deal with economic injustice, to deal with the poverty of the black people, which he knew would persist despite the civil rights laws. That was the fundamental problem and that's why in early 1968, just before his assassination, he planned for the Poor People's March on Washington. That whole record of Martin Luther King, you might say, has been kept in darkness by the establishment, and it certainly should be brought forth.

It's almost like he's frozen on the steps of the Lincoln Memorial in giving that very poetic speech. But another thing about King was what he was doing in Memphis when he was assassinated, exactly a year to the day that he gave that Riverside Church speech. He was organizing striking sanitation workers, and most people don't know about that.

You know that was a remarkable moment, the strike of the sanitation workers in Memphis, which he supported. And you're right, people know he was assassinated, but they have no idea what he was doing in Memphis. Why was he there? He was there to support these strikers. And I wonder how many of the teachers in this country who teach about Martin Luther King—and of course, everybody teaches about Martin Luther King—know why he was in Memphis or know about King and the kinds of things we were just talking about.

It seems these are the kinds of nuggets that are hidden.

I'm happy to say that there's a new generation of young historians and teachers who are taking a new approach to American history. This development is encouraging. I'm not claiming they're a majority at all, but certainly there is a substantial minority in the teaching profession. I speak all over the country and whatever town I'm in, I'm always running into teachers who are trying to teach a new kind of history to their students.

You tell a moving and inspiring story of the first time you go to south-west Georgia, and you say you thought you were almost moving back into the age of slavery. But underneath those appearances, there was something remarkable going on, in terms of organizing.

You're talking about Albany, Georgia, in 1960–61. The first sit-ins had taken place in February 1960 in Greensboro, North Carolina. And then, of course, a wave of sit-ins throughout the South in the spring of 1960. In March of 1960 it spread to Atlanta, Georgia, where I was teaching at Spelman College. Yes, things were happening, but there were parts of the South that were still silent, places the movement had not yet reached. One of these was Albany, Georgia. As you pointed out, in part of the South it felt as if slavery was still there. That was the atmosphere I felt as I went into Albany in December of 1960. I went there because there had been suddenly, surprisingly, an uprising of the black population of Albany, Georgia. I say, "suddenly and surprisingly," that is, suddenly, surprisingly to outside observers, but not surprisingly to people who lived in Albany and who knew that under the surface of silence and under the surface of obedience to the norms of segregation, the black population of Albany was seething with anger against daily humiliation. And it broke out in December of 1960 with demonstrations and sit-ins. A young woman, a kid really, a sixteen-year-old kid refusing to sit in the back of the bus and being arrested. I remember her name, Ola Mae Quarterman, a remarkable young person. The bus driver ordered her to get in the back, and she said, "I paid my damn nickel and I'll sit where I please." Thousands of young people in Albany were arrested—you might say, a good portion of the black population.

And at that point, the Southern Regional Council, which was a research organization in Atlanta, asked me if I would go down to Albany to make a report on the situation there. All of these thousands of people were in jail. I was happy to go for a number of reasons. One, I was by that time on the executive board of the Student Non-violent Coordinating Committee (SNCC). And SNCC had, in fact, sent a couple of organizers who were involved in the organization of these demonstrations in Albany. Also, several students of mine had gone to join the movement in Albany and were arrested and were in jail at the time. So you might say, as a teacher, I felt it my duty to go and see if I could visit my students in jail. While I'm romanticizing that a little, I gathered that they would let me visit my students in jail, and in fact they didn't. But I did go and discovered that there had been a good deal of organization by the NAACP and by SNCC in Albany, which resulted in this eruption in December of 1960. What I came up with in the first report I made, and then in another report I made in the spring—I was taking a look at all the arrests, the beatings, the kinds of things that took place thousands of times in the South during this period of racial segregation. Looking for the key to all that was going on, it struck me that the key to it was not southern racism but the compliance of the national government with southern racism. The collaboration of the White House and of the Justice Department with racial segregation in the South. There was a common perception among liberals and the nation in general: the South is racist; the North is different. There's racial segregation in the South, but the national government is on the side of the Negro. Of course, this wasn't true at all and this was so evident in Albany where the Constitution was being violated again and again by southern law-enforcement officers, sheriffs, and police and where the federal government, which was charged constitutionally with protecting the rights of citizens, stood by and did nothing, observed and took notes. And so as I was preparing my report, there was this moment when I was writing this about the role of the federal government and coming to the conclusion that that was the key to this story. I was teaching constitutional law in my classes at Spelman College, and so I knew fairly well that the Constitution was being violated. After all, the Fourteenth Amendment was intended to give the federal government power over what the states could do in racial matters and to protect citizens against racial discrimination, and to put the federal government behind them in that protection. So I knew that something was constitutionally wrong. I did some research and found that, in fact, there was a statute, Section 242, Title 18, of the U.S. code that made it a federal crime for any official to violate constitutional rights. And therefore the federal government should have been apprehending the sheriff of Dougherty County and the policemen of Albany. But they weren't doing a thing.

As I was preparing this report, just to check up on what I was saying in terms of the law and the Constitution, I decided to call the American Civil Liberties Union (ACLU) in New York and just get confirmation or denial of what I was concluding. So I called the ACLU. Somebody answered the phone and I said, "I'd like to talk to one of your attorneys there." And he said, "Well, I'm one of the attorneys here." I described the situation and I described what I was reporting. I said, "Does that make sense to you?" And he said, "Absolutely." I said, "By the way, what is your name?" He said, "William Kunstler." Well, Bill Kunstler was, as people came to know later, one of the important figures in the movements of the sixties, as a defense lawyer for so many people arrested in those years.

In any case, I made my report. It made the front page of the *New York Times*, and it also made the internal records of the FBI because Martin Luther King was queried by the press about what he thought of the report, which was critical of the FBI and the federal government. And he said, "That's absolutely true." The FBI, I learned this later from a Freedom of Information request, had recorded this. It was sort of an early signal to J. Edgar Hoover that King was somebody that they really had to keep an eye on, that he was a critic of the FBI. Because it was the first time he had openly said something about the FBI.

And the FBI then wiretapped him, surveilled him extensively, while simultaneously not enforcing the laws of the land.

The record of the FBI in relation to the civil rights movement was a horrendous one, and I think it's always important when talking about that, not to sort of sequester the FBI as the culprit in this because the FBI is part of the Justice Department. The attorney general is in charge of the FBI. Robert Kennedy was J. Edgar Hoover's boss. John F. Kennedy was president of the United States. Ultimately they bear the responsibility for what the FBI was doing. I had a number of experiences with the FBI, which I wrote about and which, I guess, drew the FBI's attention to me also.

What did you think about two of the icons of the liberal imagination of that period: the Kennedy brothers. Apparently Bobby Kennedy was wont to say that it was with great difficulty that he signed Hoover's request to wiretap Martin Luther King.

I'm sure it was with great difficulty, but he did it. And therefore he played a role in that really scurrilous attempt of the FBI to make Martin Luther King out to the public as someone not to be trusted. Robert Kennedy did a number of things in those years, which do not fit the image of him as a sort of champion of racial equality. Now it may have been true as some people claim that he later changed and had a better understanding of the race issue. But for a number of years he was really very much a collaborator. For instance, when the Freedom Riders were being beaten in Birmingham, Alabama, buses were being burned, the riders were being pulled out of the buses and beaten with clubs, Attorney General Robert Kennedy and the Justice Department did nothing about that. And the Freedom Riders decided, despite all of this—the bus had just been burned in Anniston, Alabama, and a number of these people were hospitalized—to go on. In fact, it was SNCC that decided to carry on the Freedom Ride that the Southern Christian Leadership Conference (SCLC) and the Congress on Racial Equality (CORE) had started, which was to carry on to Jackson, Mississippi, or to go on ahead with the original plan, which was to go all the way to New Orleans. They told the Justice Department, "We're going on to Jackson, Mississippi, what are you going to do to protect us?" Robert Kennedy, instead of saying, "Okay, you have an absolute constitutional right to ride the buses together, and the federal government is going to protect you." He made a deal with the governor of Mississippi that when they arrived in Jackson, the police would protect them from being beaten, but the police would arrest them. That was the nice liberal compromise. I remember also there was that moment when a number of black civil rights people had a meeting with Robert Kennedy to try to explain to him what was going on. They left that meeting in anger because he didn't seem to get it. As I say, later on he took a trip through the South with Marian Wright Edelman, and she gave him a little education about what was going on, and he apparently became more conscious of what was happening.

The Albany, Georgia, example is something that might inspire people today who might feel there's nothing they can do to fight the power. As you just suggested, not only was the federal government but also the state and local governments and judicial system were all against the African American citizens of that part of Georgia.

Albany was an interesting instance because the Albany experience, even by historians sympathetic to the movement, is very often looked upon as a failure. They talk about Albany, Georgia, as a failed event. I disagree very strongly with that. They consider it a failed event because it had no immediate consequences in terms of changing the situation in Albany. But it had enormous consequences in giving hope to the people in Albany and showing them that they could resist and survive. Also, it laid the seeds for later change in Albany. So I think it was a very superficial view of the situation, which happens very often, that is, momentary defeats or defeats that may not be overcome for several years are simply labeled "defeats" without understanding that very often defeats lay the groundwork for later victories because of what happens to people in the course of that struggle. I believe that's what happened in Albany. One of the SNCC people who went into Albany, Charles Sherrod, who was arrested, stayed in Albany. He's there to this day, forty years later, organizing people. When you talk to him about the Albany events, he says that that was no defeat—that was a victory for the black people of Albany.

And make the connection with people today who may feel that they have no tools to fight the power of the establishment.

Of course, it's not just Albany. The whole history of the civil rights movement is a history of people who appear to be powerless, who appear to be helpless, and who manage—by perseverance, by risk taking, by courage—to organize, to speak out, to gain adherents, to win the sympathy of people, to win support, and to finally break through and make some changes. The whole civil rights movement is an example of that.

I moved to the South in 1956, and it did seem hopeless. That is, the black people of the South had no resources to defend themselves. The federal government was against them. The local governments were against them. They did not have economic power. They had no political power. The police forces were all white. The state troopers were all white. It didn't look as if they had a chance. And yet a movement began. And nobody can say when it began. Some people trace it to the sit-ins of 1960, but you can trace it back to the Montgomery Bus Boycott of 1955. You can even trace it before that to invisible stirrings below the surface. There were bus boycotts before Montgomery that were not acknowledged, not reported. There were sit-ins before the 1960s sit-ins, which nobody took notice of. There were quiet actions that took place that were defeated. There were gatherings of black people in churches, on college campuses, and elsewhere that were preparing the way for what finally happened. The forces of segregation claimed that they would never give in; this is a common thing you see so often in history, that people who hold onto the status quo very confidently say, "We will never be defeated." The Ford Motor Company facing the strikers of the 1930s, General Motors facing its strikers in 1936–37, saying "Oh no, they can't beat us—we're too big, too strong." They were defeated. And this happened in the civil rights movement. I have this vivid memory of being at the end of the Selma to Montgomery march in 1965, and I was on the last leg of this march coming into Montgomery, and finally the march culminated in Montgomery and I went to the airport to fly back home. In fact, I encountered Whitney Young, who was head of the Urban League. Whitney Young had come down at the last moment. He hadn't participated in the march—like a lot of leaders, he came down at the last moment to participate in the ceremonies—and he was there at the airport. We were old colleagues from the Atlanta University system. We sat at a table in the restaurant, black and white together you might say, and the waitress who waited on us had this big button, which said, "The White South Says Never." And she was serving us.

One of the things I have to say for people who can't see you is the extraordinary animation that you bring to telling this story, and I know part of that is because you were there—you talked to these people, you walked those roads. And that breathes a certain kind of life into history that is not common.

One of the things that I often tell teachers is that I think they should never hesitate to bring their own personal experiences into the classroom. Teachers are very often shy about that. They think it's sort of unprofessional. You know—teach the syllabus, teach the textbook, teach the stuff that you want to teach, but don't bring in your own life and your own experiences. But after all, every teacher— maybe the teacher has not had the kind of experiences I have had— but all teachers have lived certain kinds of experiences, which made them who they are. And whatever those experiences are, whatever led to a change in consciousness of those teachers, students should know about that. And I discovered this: that whenever I brought into the classroom my own experiences, the interest of the students suddenly quickened. I don't want to say that before I brought my experiences in my students were asleep. I like to think that half of them were awake. [Laughs] But certainly when I began to bring my own life into it, my own experiences, yes students' interest always quickened. A lot of teachers don't understand this; students always want to know who their teachers are, who they really are, behind the textbook, behind the syllabus, what their lives are like, what they went through, and what they're thinking about. I always resented it when I was a student and I spent a semester or a year with a teacher and at the end of the semester and at the end of the year I didn't know where that teacher stood. I thought there was something missing there.

You can't be neutral on a moving train.

That's right. [Laughs]

That could be a title of a book.

That's a good idea. [Laughs]

Talk more about Martin Luther King. Did you ever meet him? What about his using civil disobedience as a tactic of resistance. He had gone to India and had been influenced by Gandhi.

Sometimes you take something directly from a mentor like Gandhi, and sometimes you come to a position and find it reinforced by what you read and encounter. So, very often it's hard to distinguish between those two possibilities. How much did King already have in his consciousness about the philosophy of nonviolence before he studied Gandhi? How much of it was initiated by Gandhi? How much of it was reinforced by Gandhi? But certainly there's this confluence of these two important people. I knew King simply because his family was an Atlanta family and I was teaching in Atlanta, and the black community of Atlanta was a very close-knit community. So it was inevitable that I would come into contact with King on social occasions and so on.

How did you find him as a man?

Very low-key. That is very often true of great speakers—that you meet them, and I don't know what you expect, you expect them to break out into an oration when you say, "Good morning." But no, very often they're very quiet and that's the way King was. Quiet and modest, thoughtful, measured, nothing of the charismatic leader showing in personal encounters. And we would talk about nonviolence, and I remember the issue coming up, which always comes up, how total is your belief and aren't there any situations where you might change your views? And King would say, well there might be, I don't want to take an absolutist position on this. People always ask, "Well, what if your wife was being . . ." They always bring that up. He said, "I don't know what I would do in such a situation, but I can tell you how I feel about the specific situation that we are dealing with today." Gandhi was really similar. Gandhi was not an absolutist on the question of nonviolence. He suggested that, who knows, there might be times when it would not be the right thing to be perfectly passive and nonviolent. But certainly, in the historical situation in which Gandhi found himself, and similarly for King, they thought that nonviolence was not only a good tactic but philosophically defensible. And very often this is overlooked. The establishment especially likes to overlook the philosophical basis for that and think of it only as a tactic. I think failure to understand the philosophy of nonviolence is responsible for the idea that King thought that if you were arrested, it was only right that you should go to jail and take your punishment. There's a sort of comfortable, liberal idea about civil disobedience that it's all right to commit civil disobedience, but then you must take your punishment. And of course very often the leaders of the civil rights movement took their punishment and went to jail. King did, Gandhi did. But that doesn't mean that they thought it was right to take your punishment, and it doesn't mean that under all circumstances they would have done the same. There might have been circumstances in which they would have refused to take their punishment because certainly they didn't think it was right that they should be put behind bars for what they did. I think nonviolence was a deeply held belief. I guess I should add this: that very often the word *nonviolence* is used in isolation from action, and nonviolence, and pacifism too, are considered to be passive reactions to injustice. But that was not the intention of King and Gandhi and certainly you can see that in their behavior. The phrase that King used, and the phrase that SNCC used, and the people in the southern movement used, was not simply *nonviolence* but *nonviolent direct action*. Passivity was not the answer. Action was the answer. The action would not initiate violence. The action might bring about violence inevitably because the forces in power might use violence against people who are nonviolent, but that was understood and that shouldn't stop people from engaging in nonviolent actions. But the point was that if you're going to make progress, you're going to have to take action against the establishment. You're going to have to resist it in some way, although you do it nonviolently.

It's interesting that Gandhi called it satyagraha, *which is truth force. He saw it as a very active motion, something moving forward rather than being acted upon.*

King and Gandhi were together on that point.

3

THE BACKSEAT INTERVIEW, PART II

Albuquerque/Santa Fe, New Mexico
September 18, 2002

*We're now driving back to Santa Fe after you spoke to an audience at
the University of New Mexico.*

*A lot of questions from people who are directly engaged in teaching
and who themselves are, you might say, agents of educational change
and social change in what they do. It was a good audience in terms of
gender and racial diversity.*

And you like that kind of give-and-take exchange.

I do, yes. I actually prefer it to the kind of formal lecture. It's
more fun. Because when you lecture, you're responding to what
you think are the questions in the audience. You're imagining
what questions might be, and presumably you've fashioned your
talk to respond to that. But here you don't have to imagine. These
are the questions. You're directly responding to what's on people's
minds.

*Just to go back on Gandhi and King. Here were two major social
change figures who were never elected to office.*

That tells you something, I suppose. Some of the most important figures in history have not been elected to office, and probably there's a logic to that, and that is: Once you're elected to office, you become a less important person in history. That is, you may become more important in the eyes of the establishment, in that you have the power to make decisions but less important as a factor in social change because as soon as you take office, you are being battered by all of the instruments of wealth and power, which diminish whatever moral compassion you initially brought to that office. So King didn't seek office and neither did Gandhi. You may recall that Albert Einstein was offered the presidency of Israel when Israel was first formed, and he refused it. I think he understood that the principles that he held so strongly would in some way be blunted by entering that den of corruption that exists around every political leader.

Another figure from the 1960s who made an impact, and was assassinated in 1965, was Malcolm X. What do you think of him?

Malcolm X is a very important figure, especially for young black people. And he was an important counter, you might say, to whatever tendencies there were in the civil rights movement to naïveté. He was not going to be taken in by the black establishment or the white establishment. He analyzed the March on Washington as an example of a controlled movement, a movement controlled by the powers that be. So he was a fresh and vigorous voice, saying things that other people in the movement would not say. And sure, he was an angry voice, a scary voice to white people because he talked about self-defense. He did not believe in nonviolence, although there's no indication that he ever engaged in an act of violence or provoked violence. But he certainly believed in self-defense. In fact, a number of people in the civil rights movement, who were part of what you might call the nonviolent civil rights movement, did in fact believe in self-defense. And he believed in separation. There was a certain validity to his worry that if you didn't have separation, any integrated group would be dominated by whites, the people with the most power and the most money. There's value to this position, even though it wasn't an ultimate moral position. In fact, Malcolm gave voice to this ultimate position at a certain point later in his life when he came back from Mecca, not long before his death, and he took a different view of racial segregation and was more open to black, white interchange, working together.

One of his most famous speeches is the "The house Negro vs. the field Negro." The house Negro was kowtowing and obsequious to the white plantation owner. And the field Negro was rebellious, active, and seeking to break away and to free himself.

Malcolm was great at sort of epitomizing ideas in very colorful analogies and metaphors. I remember him saying that if the master's house caught on fire, the house Negro would say, "Our house is on fire!" And the field Negro would say something like, "Great!"

Let's move on to an area that you take a lot of interest in, and that is books. There's an under-reported phenomenon going on right now in terms of bestsellers around the country. Books by Noam Chomsky, 9-11; Barbara Ehrenreich, Nickel and Dimed; Michael Moore, Stupid White Men; Kevin Phillips, Wealth and Democracy; Eric Schlosser, Fast Food Nation—all of these have a progressive bent. And they're on the bestseller list. What accounts for that?

What accounts for that, I think, is an under-reported and unnoticed large segment of the American population, which does not go along with the orthodoxy that we see at the top. That does not go along with our political leaders and does not go along with our cultural leaders in the newspaper and the television industry. It indicates that there are millions of people in this country who are dissenters. And so I think it's a very healthy bit of data that we see Noam Chomsky's book, 9-11, selling a couple of hundred thousand copies. And Barbara Ehrenreich's book is about the class situation in this country, about poor people just desperately trying to survive after the so-called welfare reform of Clinton and the Republicans. And her book, *Nickel and Dimed*, has been on the *New York Times* best-seller list for many, many weeks. That's, I think, a very good sign. And of course, Michael Moore's book has been up there on the bestseller list. He's outrageously irreverent in dealing with corporate power and military power. So all of that is a very hopeful sign, but it should also be a sign to us of how this large number of dissenting Americans can be ignored. But they're there.

Independent publishers such as Seven Stories and South End Press are doing well.

That's another good sign, especially since these last several decades have seen a centralization of the publishing industry, where the publishers have been merging and merging and merging until we have industrial giants controlling the publishing industry. I remember being shocked myself when I learned that the publisher of my *People's History of the United States*, HarperCollins, was now owned by Murdoch. And you have Viacom and Disney owning publishing mega enterprises. So the fact that the independent small publishers that are managing to survive—and even as you pointed out, grow— and sell a lot of books, is a sign that despite this monopolization that has been taking place, there's a hunger out there for different voices. You mentioned Seven Stories and South End. There are also The New Press and Beacon Press. The latter is independent of corporate power, it's run by the Unitarian Universalist Church. And they're open to all sorts of books. At least what we have now are books we can point young people to and say, "Here's something you can read."

Talk about the value of literature and the printed word. Particularly in a time where it seems that cinema has become a dominant cultural force. For example, you ask someone, "Did you read The English Patient *by the Canadian writer Michael Ondaatje?" And they say, "No I didn't read the book, but I saw the movie." Did you read Harper Lee's* To Kill a Mockingbird? *And they say the exact same thing.*

I sometimes say that myself. [Laughs] But most of the time I do read the book before I see the movie, and most always I am disappointed because if you have a really good book, movies will rarely do justice to it. There are very rare exceptions. *The Spy Who Came in from the Cold* was a remarkable movie made out of a very good John le Carré book. But to answer your question more directly about the relative value of books and the visual media, obviously many, many more millions of people see movies than read books. But that doesn't tell you anything about the quality of the impact, the depth of the influence. I'd often use this test to confirm my belief, hardly based on scientific inquiry. Hardly any of my beliefs are based on scientific inquiry. But as a test of my belief that the visual media, as sensational and glamorous and mesmerizing as they can be, do not have the lasting influence that books have, I use this simple test. Many people have told me, "I read this book and it changed my life." Many people have told me that about various books. Nobody has ever said that to me about a film. I've never heard anyone say, "This film changed my life." That also is sobering for me, who is interested in movies, and who would actually like to see movies made of things that I've written. But it sobers me when I'm at first captivated by the thought, "Oh my God, maybe A *People's History of the United States* could be put on the screen and seen by ten million people. Instead of being read by one million people." Yes, ten million people is a larger number than one million. You may notice that my mathematics is of a higher sort. But I'm dubious that if A *People's History* was put on screen, it would have as important an effect on viewers as the book has had on readers.

Books are read, and reread, referred to, and underlined.

You go back to a book, and you play with a book, and you sit and stand and sleep with a book. And you can rewind the book, very easily.

You say that books are still the freest area of inquiry. What do you mean by that?

Despite the fact that the publishing industry has become so dominated by multinational giants, there's still more leeway for writing unorthodox books. And even books that are published by commercial publishers, because even commercial publishers are interested in money. And if they think Michael Moore's book will make money, well then, HarperCollins will publish it, as they have. And they have made money. So, it's a trade-off; they're willing to give Michael Moore his moment so long as they can reap the profits. So, I think pointing people to books is a very good idea. Otherwise, they are enslaved by television or *Time, Newsweek,* or their local newspaper.

Another part of the unreported resistance that's going on right now is the enormous demands made on people like you and Noam Chomsky and Angela Davis to give public talks. And there are these huge crowds that turn out.

I think certainly that's yet another good sign. That Michael Moore might draw five thousand people. Thousands of people turn out for Noam Chomsky. I will talk in Santa Cruz, and two thousand people will show up. What these packed audiences mean, I think, is that all over the country—and this happens not just in major cities, it happens very often in small towns—there are people hungry for information that they don't get in the traditional sources.

A People's History of the United States was initially under contract by Rupert Murdoch's News Corporation, Fox, and now it's at HBO, which is actually controlled by AOL–Time Warner. What's the status of the TV project?

The project, which Fox first undertook then dropped, not to my surprise, was to take episodes out of the book and dramatize them in full-length feature films for television. Fox toyed with it for a while. Four of us were going to be executive producers: Matt Damon, Ben Affleck, Chris Moore, and myself. We deliberately set ourselves up that way so that we could have some control over what was being done. But Fox dropped it; HBO took it up. We were actually glad that HBO took it up—even though HBO, as you pointed out, has its ultimate boss as AOL–Time Warner—because HBO seems to be freer and bolder than other networks. That's probably because it has no commercials, it has no advertisers to deal with. So, at this point, HBO has commissioned two writers—writers whom we, the executive producers, chose. Writers to write films based on two episodes in the book. We have one writer writing a script on the Columbus Las Casas story, and we have another writer writing a script on the American Revolution, an irreverent look at the American Revolution. So the scripts are being written. If HBO likes the scripts, well, they'll be turned into movies. If HBO doesn't like the scripts, they'll be turned into. . . .

[Postscript: Since this interview, HBO has dropped the project. I don't know why. Perhaps it was because it was dauntingly huge. Perhaps because the scripts that were turned in were not, as John Sayles put it, having written one of them, "sexy enough."]

The Sopranos *is a popular HBO series. And, in one episode, the mobster's son is seen reading a certain book by a certain historian.*

Somebody who saw that episode of *The Sopranos* told me about it. Tony Soprano's son, who is in school, is sitting in the kitchen and he has before him a copy of *A People's History of the United States*. He is confronted by Tony Soprano, and I think also by Tony Soprano's wife, because he apparently has been telling them that he is reading his schoolbook, *A People's History*, which tells him that Columbus murdered, kidnapped, and tortured Indians. His father, Tony Soprano, who's not the most enlightened person in the world, goes into a kind of minor rage. There are a few moments of conflict between the son and his parents. The son says, "Look, this is what my teacher says, and this is what my book says." And Tony Soprano says, "I don't care what your teacher says, and I don't care what your book says," because Tony Soprano doesn't care what anybody says.

He has the power, right? He says, "To me, Columbus will always be a hero." They tell me that's the end of the episode.

The opening scene of The Godfather *is interesting. The supplicant comes to the Don, who is played by Marlon Brando, and needs a favor. Brando lays out his terms. Then the supplicant agrees to obey the godfather and kisses him on the hand. It seems to me that might be a good way to explain how U.S. foreign policy works. That if you play along with the Don, you're honored and protected. And if you step out of line, as they say on* The Sopranos, *fuggedaboudit.*

I feel that there's a lot of deception and self-deception in the arts practiced by people who are so anxious to see something sensible said in the arts. And it may be, of the twenty million people who see *The Sopranos*, there are two hundred people, and you are among that chosen few, who say, "Oh this is wonderful, this exposes American foreign policy!" And then there are the millions that say, "Well, that's the way the world operates, and you've got to just recognize that as a fact, and there's not much we can do about it." I have this argument with friends of mine who love *The Sopranos*. And I can understand loving something that is well done, dramatic. I saw *The Godfather*, and I admire the way it was made. There's wonderful acting—Marlon Brando, of course—and the music, the cinematography, and an exciting story. But in the end, after all of that admiration, I really worry that basically a thug and a killer, a mobster, has been humanized in such a way as to almost exonerate what he does. So, I have this complicated view of *The Godfather* and *The Sopranos*. And I will still watch *The Sopranos* for the sheer fun of it, but I will have this little voice inside saying, "Beware."

A cinema classic is Orson Welles's Citizen Kane. *It was loosely based on the life of William Randolph Hearst, the notorious newspaper baron.*

It's a very powerful and arresting movie, and all the ideologues of the cinema, all the people who love to analyze cinema, point to all the innovations, all the camera work and so on. And all of that is true. I learned about Hearst long before I saw *Citizen Kane.* I read a book by Ferdinand Lundberg, called *Imperial Hearst.* You can imagine what his point of view was. When I was learning about the Spanish American War, I learned about Hearst's role in beefing up public opinion to support the war. To me, Hearst was always one of the evil men. In that sense, a film that is somewhat based on Hearst, and which people understood was based on Hearst, is, I suppose, a socially useful film. Again, there's always a problem when you take an important idea and turn it into a work of art. There's always a problem as to whether the ultimate product fulfills your initial aim. Now I'm not sure what the initial aim of Orson Welles was, but I suspect that since he was a political person with ideas, he had an ideological aim. What was the effect of *Citizen Kane* on the millions of people who saw it? The truth is I don't know. I don't immediately jump into the chorus that says, "Oh, the greatest film of all time!" But it was a good film.

Some people are making comparisons between what is going on today politically and George Orwell's 1984. *With a permanent war going on in the background, the citizens of Oceana don't even know who's fighting where anymore, and there's an enormous government security apparatus. Big Brother is watching. The Ministry of Truth has a memory hole into which inconvenient facts are dropped. The Ministry of Truth has on the side of its white pyramidal-shaped building the slogans of the party: "War is Peace," "Freedom is Slavery," "Ignorance is Strength." What kind of parallels do you see between the current situation with the war on terrorism and that kind of totalitarian landscape that Orwell drew?*

Orwell's 1984 is an accurate and troubling guide to what we are seeing today: the control of public opinion, the manipulation of language, the slogans that are used, names that are given to horrible foreign policy actions, names that are given to bombings and wars. Afghanistan was at first called "Operation Infinite Justice," then they changed it to "Operation Enduring Freedom." Where is the freedom involved in bombing a country that has been bombed and bombed and bombed? A country of desperate, miserable, starving people. Where is the freedom involved in that? And the language. The word *security* has been used again and again. All of these measures being taken to control our information, to give more powers to the FBI, the police, and the security apparatus. All for security. It all presupposes that it makes Americans more secure. But how does more and more interference in your private life and in your conversations, in what you say and what you do, make you more secure? And how does a war make the people in this country more secure, if that war in fact is likely to inflame terrorism in the world? What about the security of other countries? The word *security* is bounded by nationalism. It doesn't take in the security of other countries. So when you bomb another country, you're not particularly considering the security of people in that country. But that isn't part of the message when the word *security* is used. So yes, there's an absolutely Orwellian use of language here by the Bush administration. The Bush administration is not the first to use euphemisms to cover up horrendous deeds. But it is now taking Orwell's 1984 probably further than ever.

We're in New Mexico driving back to Santa Fe. As you look out on this landscape, are you reminded of its very unusual history? Perhaps even the first 9/11 was on this soil. Today many Native Americans are confined to reservations where they're allowed to sell cheap cigarettes and alcohol and to operate casinos in order to support themselves. This state also has had a major connection with the military industrial complex. The first atomic bomb was developed and tested here. Los Alamos Labs, which is near Santa Fe, designs weapons of mass destruction.

You're doing several things here. You're bringing up the history of New Mexico, a complicated history. A history that can be very instructive. One of the first things that people should know about the history of New Mexico is that it belonged to Mexico. There's a reason why it was called New Mexico. It was taken as the spoils of war. It was taken in an aggressive war fought by the United States between 1846 and 1848—a war of conquest. New Mexico is part of the spoils of that war. So the origins of New Mexico as an American territory, and then an American state, should be understood as part of the history of American expansionism and imperialism. And then, of course, New Mexico is used, as you point out, as a military base and is used to construct the atomic bomb. How ironic that the United States is prepared to go to war against Iraq and bomb Iraq because Iraq may have weapons of mass destruction. We are going to use weapons of mass destruction against a country because we think it may have weapons of mass destruction. The United States has more weapons of mass destruction than anyone and has used them with more deadly effect than any other country in the world. So you have this irony connected with our accusations against Saddam Hussein, who indeed may have had weapons of mass destruction, but they pale in size and importance compared to what the United States possesses and what the United States has done with those weapons.

And the situation of Native Americans?

Native Americans have been marginalized and are still, very often, living in poverty and on Indian land, on reservations. A few of them have become prosperous, and the prosperity of those few have often been pointed out as an example of how well the Indians are doing. But most of them are not doing well. Theirs is a kind of invisible culture inside the United States. A culture that is being deprived of the great benefits that this rich country could give to them if it chose to do so. On the other hand, there's an Indian movement, a movement of resistance, an organization of Indians who are trying to fight back, who are trying to educate the country about their situation and, by organization and agitation, to change their condition.

4

WAR ON IRAQ: A DISSENTING VIEW

KGNU, Boulder, Colorado
March 25, 2003

Why do you dissent from the Bush administration position that its attack on Iraq is justified?

My dissent is based on something that is not hard to see. And that is that Iraq does not and did not pose any imminent threat to the United States or to anybody else. Iraq was not threatening anybody, was not attacking anybody, was not invading anybody. Therefore, this was an assault by the United States that was unprovoked, an act of aggression, the kind of thing that when done by other countries in the past has brought international outrage. When Hitler marched into other countries, when Japan marched into other countries, this was looked upon as unspeakable. You don't simply decide you're going to go into another country because you don't like the way they're ruled or because—as in, I think, this case—you really want to plant some of your power in that part of the world. None of the excuses given by the Bush administration for going to war in Iraq have held up.

I think that's the reason for the enormous outpouring of protest against the war. That's the reason why on February 15, 2003, perhaps ten million people around the world demonstrated against the

United States going to war in Iraq. I think the reason for this enormous protest, both abroad and here in this country—unprecedented really in this country at such an early stage in any war—is that the Bush administration's rationale for going to war was so obviously empty, so obviously false, and so clearly concealed motives it was not willing to admit. Instead, the Bush administration resorted to claims that, upon just a little examination, could be perceived to be false.

The idea, for instance, that Iraq had weapons of mass destruction and that this was an occasion for war. The other countries in the world, indeed the other nations in the Security Council, which had the job of overseeing the disarmament of Iraq after the Gulf War, obviously were not going along with the United States on this issue. The UN inspectors were there. They couldn't find any weapons of mass destruction.

It became kind of absurd because every time the United States made a demand, Iraq complied, and it was never enough. First, the United States said, Oh, will you allow the inspectors in? Yes. Oh, but will you allow them to have unfettered access? Yes. Will you allow them to look through the presidential palaces? Yes. Will you allow overflights? Yes. Will you allow interviews with scientists? Yes. Nothing would satisfy the Bush administration. So it became clear that the Bush administration was not really interested in the issue of weapons of mass destruction. They just wanted to invade Iraq.

And just another note on weapons of mass destruction: There is something absurd about thinking that even if Iraq did possess weapons of mass destruction—and in fact it did not—it posed a unique threat. There were eight other countries in the world that had nuclear weapons. The United States wasn't talking about making war with them. And who had more nuclear weapons than the United States? Ten thousand nuclear weapons held by the United States.

There was an enormous hypocrisy in this charge of weapons of mass destruction.

Then there is the whole business of, well, they violated Security Council resolutions, which in fact they did. Iraq did violate Security Council resolutions. So have other countries. Israel has violated Security Council resolutions. The United States has violated Security Council resolutions. The United States has exercised its veto over Security Council resolutions perhaps a hundred times or more. When you use your veto, you don't have to violate a Security Council resolution, you just veto it. So that charge about violation was also an act of hypocrisy.

And then, well, he's a tyrant. He tyrannizes his people. True, absolutely true. So do many, many other tyrants in the world, a number of them allies of the United States. There are countries in the world that are ruled by cruel regimes, like Saddam Hussein, which tyrannize their own people. You can't simply decide that you are going to solve all these problems of tyranny by war, which is what the United States claims to be doing in this instance. But, again, hypocrisy. Take Algeria. Algeria has been engaged in enormous killing of dissidents, thousands and thousands of people. But, in fact, an assistant secretary of state for Mideastern affairs for the United States said at one point after September 11, we could learn something from Algeria in dealing with the problem of terrorism. If you look down the list of countries put out by Amnesty International, countries that are guilty of torture, of the execution of dissidents, Saudi Arabia is very high on the list, and there are many, many other countries. So the charge that we're going to war because Hussein is a tyrant clearly doesn't make any sense.

Then there is something else to consider. If indeed Saddam Hussein is tyrannizing his people—and he is—when you make war against a tyrant, what are you doing? You are killing the victims of the tyrant. Who are the people who are dying in this war right now? They're the ordinary people of Iraq, ordinary civilians, ordinary soldiers. By the way, I don't make a distinction between innocent civilians and guilty soldiers. All of these people who are dying are innocent. Their soldiers and our soldiers who are dying are innocent in the sense that they're all young people who were either conscripted, as in Iraq, or cajoled and seduced into joining the military, as in this country. They don't want to die. But these are the people who die in war, not the leaders of the country.

In any case, all of these claims made by the United States about why we're going to war in Iraq immediately disintegrate as soon as you begin to examine them, which then leads you to ask the question, What are the real motives of the United States in going into Iraq, the motives that they're not telling us about?

What are those motives?

The motives are really all connected with something that is a historic fact for Western civilization—I'll put civilization in quotes—and for the United States. And that is, this period of modern times from the fifteenth century to now has been a period of Western imperial expansion into the so-called backward areas of the earth, into the Third World countries, into places too weak to defend themselves, places that had rich stores of raw materials, whether it's rubber in Southeast Asia or gold in the Belgian Congo, or whether it's oil in the Middle East, cotton in India and Egypt. There is a long history of imperial expansion into such countries.

The United States entered that imperial race rather late—that is, roughly at the beginning of the twentieth century—but entered it very decisively, by first going into Cuba, presumably liberating Cuba from Spain but actually planting American power in Cuba. American corporations, American banks, American railroads, moved in as soon as Spain was ousted, and they fundamentally controlled Cuba until Castro's revolution of 1959. Also, in the early part of the twentieth century, the United States moved out into the Pacific and took over Hawaii. It took over the Philippines in a very bloody war of imperial conquest.

What I am arguing is that what is going on now in Iraq is a continuation of the long, long history of American expansion in the world. It's a process that starts right after the American Revolution, expanding across the continent to the Pacific, fighting a war with Mexico—I should say, more accurately, instigating a war with Mexico—and then taking almost half of Mexico, that whole southwest part of what is now the United States, and driving the hundreds of Indian tribes out of their land, fighting bloody wars, committing massacres against the Indians. All for expansion. I talked about the turn of the century. After that, the United States Marines again and again went into the Caribbean and Central America, occupying Haiti, the Dominican Republic, and Nicaragua for many years.

And then, after World War II, the United States becomes the great superpower in the world, along with the Soviet Union. But the United States now has really taken over from the old Western empires—England and France, for instance—control of Mideast oil. And not all of it, because there have been attempts by nations in the Middle East to remove oil reserves from the control of the United States. But when they do that, they run into trouble.

In 1953, when a nationalist leader in Iran, Mossadegh, nationalized the oil fields, that could not be tolerated. It's interesting to hear Bush say, We'll give the oil fields back to the Iraqis. No, the oil fields have always been the target of attention of American corporations. And in 1953 Mossadegh was overthrown and the shah of Iran was put in. The shah of Iran was going to be generous with American oil corporations. And this situation now in Iraq, if we get rid of Saddam Hussein and we come in there, then we will control the oil reserves of Iraq. So imperial expansion connected with a control of vital materials, that has had a long history. And I believe that what is happening now in Iraq is a continuation of that history.

Oil drives the U.S. economy and the global economy. And Iraq, after Saudi Arabia, has the largest oil reserves in the world. As someone commented rather rhetorically, If Iraq grew grapefruit and bananas, do you think the United States would invade it?

That's a good question. I think a lot of people in this country are deceived by that whole question, because there are people who say, Well, we need oil. Of course, we do need oil. But there are two questions to be asked. One is, Do we need Mideast oil? It's been estimated that if the United States government would only regulate automobile emissions in a more serious way than it has, then we would not need any oil from the Middle East. And then there is another point to be made. If these nations control their own oil—if Iraq and Iran control their own oil—are they going to withhold it from the rest of the world? No, they must sell it. There is no point in holding onto it. There is nothing they can do with it. They must sell it. But they will sell it at their prices. And ultimately the real issue is not whether we have the oil. The real issue is the price of oil. Thomas Friedman, a regular *New York Times* columnist who appears a lot on radio and television, has certainly been a supporter of this war against Iraq. I remember that just before the first Gulf War, Friedman said, You know what this war is about—he was being very honest—it's about the price of oil. Not about the control of oil but the price of oil.

So, yes, I see this war against Iraq as part of that continuing American interest in the oil of the Middle East, an interest that became very real in 1945 at the end of World War II, when Franklin D. Roosevelt met with Ibn Saud of Saudi Arabia. They basically came to a kind of deal. And the deal was that the United States would move into these areas of the Middle East, which had formerly been dominated by England and France, both of them now rather racked by the war. In return, the United States would guarantee the security of the Saudi Arabian monarchy, a backward and semifeudal monarchy, which persists to this day and which the United States protects to this day despite the fact that the cruelties inflicted by the Saudi regime on its own population, particularly its women, are not very far from what goes on in Iraq or from what happened in Afghanistan under the Taliban.

Fifteen of the nineteen hijackers on September 11 were from Saudi Arabia, and Saudi Arabia financed the Afghan mujahideen, who then morphed into the Taliban. Elements in the kingdom have had ties with al-Qaeda.

It's interesting how the media in the United States has so misinformed the American public or has been so complicit in keeping the American public ignorant, as the government has been really intent on doing, that most Americans think that Iraq was somehow involved in September 11. There is no proof at all that Iraq was involved. And, as you say, most of the hijackers were from Saudi Arabia, a country that is our ally.

So this point that I just made about the media and misinformation is something that's very, very troubling, because I believe that if the American people were really informed about what has been going on in the Middle East, if they really were informed about the history of the Middle East—and some of that history that you just supplied about the connections with al-Qaeda, with Osama bin Laden, with the Taliban—if the American people knew some of that history, if they knew how much the United States had to do with keeping Saddam Hussein in power, with giving him chemical and biological weapons in the 1980s when he was fighting against Iran, if the American people knew some of this history, we wouldn't have this support for the war that the polls tell us a majority of the people in the United States express. I think if the American people were given information, were given some of the history, were given, for instance, the history of American expansion in the world, I think that they would not be in support of this war.

A few years ago, a study showed that the more people watch television, the less they actually know about public affairs.

That's interesting. There is a kind of maverick media person named Danny Schechter who wrote a book called *The More You Watch, the Less You Know.* And, yes, it's certainly true. Unfortunately, television is the main source of information for so many Americans, and television is so much the handmaiden of corporate America and the government. I have found a few exceptions. C-SPAN, I've noticed since the war started, has been giving some attention to people who dissent from the war policy of the Bush administration, and it's given us some reports from the foreign press, which we don't get here in the United States.

One of the major themes among pro-war advocates turns on the whole experience of the late 1930s and early 1940s. So there were constant references to Hitler, Munich, appeasement, Chamberlain, and the

League of Nations. The major book that brings up that past is The Threatening Storm: The Case for Invading Iraq *by Kenneth Pollack, a former Clinton National Security Council staff member and former CIA analyst. This book even influenced the so-called liberal* New Yorker *magazine, which came out with a pro-war editorial. How effective do you think those kinds of images are in swaying public opinion, that if the United States "gives in" to Saddam, since he's like Hitler, this would be tantamount to Munich, and then things will get even worse?*

It's a very effective and seductive argument. I think it's a terribly misleading and false argument, but as far as its effectiveness, I have no doubt it's effective, simply because World War II is still a good war in the minds of most Americans. Therefore, it's been devilishly clever on the part of the United States government—and the media in large part has gone along with this—to constantly bring in World War II as an analogy to whatever the United States was doing, so that that glow of goodness around World War II was transplanted to every ugly war that we have fought since World War II. Every enemy of the United States was Hitler, and any attempt to say that we should not go to war was looked upon as appeasement. In Vietnam, Ho Chi Minh was compared to Hitler, and not to fight in Vietnam was to be considered appeasing the Communists. So in the name of not appeasing the Communists, we fought a long and bloody war in Vietnam, which resulted in the deaths of several million people, including fifty-eight thousand Americans. It's a dangerous and deadly analogy because it immediately sweeps everybody into the orbit of World War II goodness.

One of the most ludicrous examples of this is when Noriega of Panama was declared to be another Hitler. Here is tiny, tiny Panama. And here is this petty dictator, leader of the country, Noriega.

And he is being compared to Hitler. And in 1989 the United States invades Panama. This is under the elder Bush. And that little war is now sort of forgotten, and I notice that nobody brings it up; nobody in the press brings it up. But it should not be forgotten because it's an example of how the Hitler analogy is used and distorted, because what it led to in our invasion of Panama was the deaths of we don't know how many people in Panama. One thousand people, two thousand people? We know that neighborhoods were destroyed and ruined, and thousands of people were left homeless as a result of the American attack on Panama.

And by the way, it was in some respects similar to what is going on in Iraq—by "some respects," I mean there was no provocation—Panama was no danger to the United States; Noriega was no danger to the United States. So the United States engaged in an unprovoked attack. In fact, it was condemned by the Security Council, and the United States vetoed the condemnation so that the United States could not be seen as violating a Security Council resolution, only vetoing it.

But the Hitler analogy was really responsible for building up support for American wars in situations very, very different from World War II. And look at the present situation in Iraq, comparing Saddam Hussein to Hitler. They're alike in certainly one respect: They're both tyrannical rulers, and they've both engaged in acts of terrible cruelty against their own population. But there is an enormous difference, which has to do with the question of whether you go to war. Hitler was invading and attacking countries around him, swallowing them up. He was engaged in aggressive warfare against other countries, wars that he initiated. Saddam Hussein is not initiating any wars, not engaged in any warfare at the time when we decide to go to war with him. He was not attacking anybody.

In fact, oddly enough, the United States is in the same position that Hitler was in. The United States is doing the attacking. The United States is engaged in moving its troops into another country, which has not attacked it and is about to take over that country, claiming, of course, that it will bring peace and prosperity and democracy to that country. I would say that if you're going to have an analogy with Hitler, the analogy better fits our unprovoked attack on Iraq than it fits whatever Saddam Hussein is doing.

To just continue with the World War II period, U.S. Supreme Court Justice Robert Jackson was the chief U.S. prosecutor at the Nuremberg tribunal, which was convened to try the surviving Nazi leadership. And he said this: "We must make clear to the Germans that the wrong for which their fallen leaders are on trial is not that they lost the war but that they started it. And we must not allow ourselves to be drawn into a trial of the causes of the war, for our position is that no grievances or policies will justify resort to aggressive war. It is utterly renounced and condemned as an instrument of policy." The planning and waging of aggressive war are in the UN charter. Ramsey Clark, former attorney general of the United States under Lyndon Johnson, and others say that the Bush first strike on Iraq violated international law and the UN charter. What do you think about that?

Ramsey Clark is absolutely right. That's why all of the talk about, Well, Saddam Hussein is violating Security Council resolutions, is irrelevant. Yes, true. But the United States, by engaging in an unprovoked aggressive war against Iraq is violating the UN charter, which was adopted in San Francisco in 1945 and ratified by the United States. And if I remember, Article I, Section 4 of the charter says that the members of the UN shall refrain from the threat or use of force against any other state. And this invasion of Iraq is a very clear violation of the UN charter and, yes, a violation of the principles enunciated at Nuremberg, which brought about the prosecution of the leaders of Nazi Germany.

And I would argue that if there was an impartial tribunal put together in the future to judge war crimes, I think the members of the Bush administration would have to be brought before this tribunal. In fact, an international war crimes tribunal has just been set up, and you may recall that the United States insisted that it had to be exempt from the jurisdiction of this International Criminal Court. And we now know why. Because if the United States was to be considered within the purview of this International Criminal Court, then what it has done by making war on Iraq would immediately be cause for bringing it before the court and charging it with the crime of starting an unprovoked war.

The Bush administration constantly evokes the horrifying images of September 11 to essentially justify its foreign policies.

September 11 was an unquestionable act of terrorism, and, of course, it has caused enormous grief and suffering among all those thousands of people who lost somebody in the Twin Towers and the Pentagon. But then the question remains, Therefore, what do you do? What is the proper response to that? The immediate response of the Bush administration was to declare a war on terrorism and to start that war with the bombing of Afghanistan.

This seems exactly the wrong response to what happened on September 11. The wrong response for a number of reasons. One of them is that it simply was not going to have any effect on terrorism because you can't make war on terrorism in the way you make war on a specific country that you know is the source or you think is the source of your problem. Because terrorism does not stem from any one country that you can then make war on. Terrorism comes from many, many different sources. In fact, the Bush administration itself has acknowledged this. In Bush's State of the Union Address, he said—ironically, after he had just said we are winning the war on terrorism—there are tens of thousands of trained terrorists around the world and terrorists in at least a dozen countries. If that's so, then how can you make war on terrorism? So what we did in bombing Afghanistan was not to make war on terrorism but to single out some spot on earth that we could bomb with impunity, and we picked out this ravaged country, which had gone through so many years of war and misery, and bombed it, presumably to show that we were doing something about terrorism. But we were not. In fact, if anything, we were increasing the likelihood of terrorism by provoking the anger of people in the Middle East, who saw what we were doing in Afghanistan as a cruel act.

Which brings me to the second point about the Bush reaction to September 11. And that is, the United States government was reacting to an act of terrorism by its own act of terrorism, because I consider that the bombing of Afghanistan was an act of terrorism. War is terrorism. War is terrorism on a very large scale. In fact, you can, I think, see that the terrorist acts committed by groups, whether it's the IRA or suicide bombers here and there, al-Qaeda, in scale are very small compared to the acts of war committed by nations. And so the United States, in bombing Afghanistan for a year and killing thousands of people—nobody knows exactly how many civilians were killed in the bombing. Was it three thousand? Was it five thousand? Mark Herrold, an economics professor in New Hampshire, who did a lot of very meticulous scanning of the accounts of the bombing, came up with figures of from three thousand to five thousand. That was meeting terrorism with terrorism. If terrorism is the killing of innocent people for some presumed political purpose, then the killing of these thousands of people in Afghanistan presumably wanting to do something about terrorism, was itself terrorism.

I might point out that there were and are family members who lost brothers and sisters and sons and daughters and husbands and wives in the September 11 tragedy, who have organized into a group called Families for Peaceful Tomorrows. These are people who, as soon as the bombing of Afghanistan began, said: This is the wrong thing to do. We do not want our loved ones and their deaths to be avenged by causing deaths in some remote part of the world. I remember a woman named Amber Amundsen, whose husband, a pilot, was in the Pentagon when it was attacked and who was killed. And she said, My husband would not have wanted his death to be responded to by causing the deaths of other people.

So the reaction of the government to September 11 has been really horrendous. It's been immoral. It's been impractical in terms of doing something about terrorism, and it's been really a way of deflecting the attention of the public from the fact that the Bush administration does not want to do anything serious about terrorism. If it wanted to do something serious about terrorism, something that might well be effective, it might consider—and this is much more difficult than bombing a country—dealing with the roots of terrorism. And the roots of terrorism are in the grievances that huge numbers of people in various parts of the world, especially the Middle East, feel against the foreign policy of the United States. Millions of people have those grievances: grievances against the bullying of other countries by American political and economic power, grievances against the stationing of American troops in over a hundred countries in the world, grievances against the American policy in supporting Israel's occupation of the West Bank and Gaza. These are genuine grievances. Millions of people feel those grievances, and out of those millions of people, a handful will become fanatical enough to become terrorists. But unless you deal with those grievances, you are not going to be able to solve the problem of terrorism. As long as the grievances exist—you can bomb, invade, attack country after country—terrorism will still be there, threatening us.

The United States is now spending over a billion dollars a day on the military, and America spends more on weapons than most of the countries in the world combined. Bush has just asked for an additional seventy-five billion dollars just to cover the Iraq war, and no one believes that that figure is anywhere near the amount that is going to be required. The United States is the number-one arms dealer in the world, with such companies as Lockheed Martin, Northrop Grumman, Raytheon, Boeing, and General Dynamics leading the way. Political analyst Kevin Phillips warns that the United States is becoming "a garrison state"?

Well, this has been going on for some time.

But it seems to have accelerated since September 11.

Certainly since September 11 it's become much worse. We are becoming that monster that we dreaded to become. We looked at other countries in the world that were militarized, and No, we said, we're not like that. But here we are. As you say, our arms budget exceeds the combined arms budgets of most of the countries in the world. What's happening is that the enormous wealth that we have is being taken away from the American people and being devoted to war, going into the huge profits of the manufacturers of nuclear weapons and jet planes and attack helicopters, at the expense of the American people. We, the American people, the American taxpayers, all of us, are paying for this. And what's happening is that there is no money left to deal with the essential human needs of people in this country. What has been concealed by the war talk and the preparations for war, and now the ongoing war, is the fact that while all this money is going into the war, there is no money for education, no money for health, no money for child care. Cuts are being made in the Bush budget for all of the essential things that people need.

I saw an item a few weeks ago on the front page of the *New York Times*, although, like so many things that appear in the press, it appears one day and then disappears, not giving people a chance to focus on it and think about it and see its significance. But I couldn't help thinking about this, even after the news item had disappeared from the press. That is, this was an item about the fact that the Bush administration was cutting back on free school lunches for children. To me, this is a horrifying thought, that there is money for more and more weapons to fight an aggressive war in the Middle East, and there is no money for school lunches for children. This, to me, is a sort of symbol of what is happening to this country.

I was looking at some factual information given out recently by the Children's Defense Fund in Washington. The Children's Defense Fund has been working for years and years on behalf of the rights of children and the needs of children, lobbying desperately in Congress for more money to deal with the fact that one out of every five children in this country is born in poverty. And the statistics they gave out were very, very troubling about what is happening to the lives of children who are not being given adequate education, not being given adequate medical care, and therefore so many of them are dying before the age of five or growing up sick, certainly growing up poor. All of this while we are spending hundreds of billions of dollars for the military. This is something that the American people should not be tolerating.

Why do you think they tolerate it?

I think one reason they tolerate it is that they don't know about it. They really aren't made aware. Sure, the Children's Defense Fund can put out reports that will be read by a few thousand people, but the press is all full of news about the war. War is always useful for political leaders because a war enables them to conceal from the public what they are doing or not doing for the people of the country. So I think the American people, yes, are tolerating it because they, in large part, aren't made aware of it, and they're not being given the information. Their eyes are being directed toward the warplanes going over Iraq, and meanwhile their own lives are being affected in a very bad way by these distorted priorities of the Bush administration.

How do you respond to those who say: We are at war. The time for protest is over. Our men and women in uniform are in harm's way. It's time to rally around the flag and support the troops and the commander in chief?

Support the troops. It depends on what you mean by "support the troops." Do you support the troops by sending them halfway around the world to face death or wounds or the sickness that very often accompanies wars, sickness that persists even after they return from war? Is that supporting them? I see signs held by some of the protesters, and some of these signs say SUPPORT OUR GIs, BRING THEM HOME. I think that's a legitimate slogan. That's the best way to support them. But to say that we should now, because we're at war, keep quiet and let the war go on, in other words, put these young people into harm's way and keep them there until we've achieved some sort of spurious military victory, is that supporting them? Is Bush supporting the young people of our country by sending them to war, by sending them to kill and to be killed, to really poison their moral sense? This is what war does: War corrupts the moral sense of everybody who engages in it. So is Bush supporting our troops by doing that?

As for keeping quiet, this is exactly the time when we need debate. It's exactly the time when we need discussion. It's not the time to keep quiet and simply let something that is immoral and unjustified continue without any opposition. This is, I think, a very common notion, that when you're at war, dissent should stop, which is a strange kind of idea because it means that when things get most serious, when you're dealing with matters of life and death, then you don't talk anymore. What does that mean? That we have freedom of speech only when we're discussing less important things; and when we are discussing the most urgent things of all, whether people live or die, that at that point we stop discussing, arguing, debating? This is precisely the time when we need lively and democratic debate and discussion, more than ever before, because people are dying, Iraqis are dying, Americans are dying. And we should raise the level of discussion, raise the level of protest to the point where the war stops.

How can that debate and discussion take place when there is a chilling atmosphere in the country? You've written the foreword to a new book by Nancy Chang, entitled Silencing Political Dissent. *The focus of the book is on the Patriot Act, which was passed by huge majorities in the Congress after September 11. You call it "a draconian law worthy of a police state."*

In wartime—and we've had this experience before—Congress immediately passes laws that in essence abolish the Bill of Rights, abolish the First Amendment, abolish the Fourth Amendment, the right to be free from search and seizure, and, yes, exactly when we need these rights most. And we are seeing the Justice Department in the hands of Ashcroft picking up people who come from certain countries. This is guilt by association. Just because you come from a certain country, that means that now you must be treated differently from anybody else. People who are not citizens are being picked up and detained. They're not being given any trials. They're not being allowed to seek lawyers. They're being deprived of the most fundamental constitutional rights.

I think this is a very dangerous thing. Democracy is in terrible peril, precisely because in wartime they want people to keep quiet. They want to intimidate people. And it's exactly at a time like this, when the government is trying to intimidate the population into silence so that it can carry on its war without criticism, that people need to speak up and to criticize and to demand that the promises of this country and the Bill of Rights—of freedom of speech and freedom of assembly—that those promises be fulfilled. Otherwise, we don't have a democratic state. Otherwise, we are living in a police state.

Eqbal Ahmad, the brilliant Pakistani scholar/activist, always stressed the need to think strategically about goals and ways to achieve them. Talk about civil disobedience and nonviolence as a tactic and strategy of resistance. You've engaged in civil disobedience. You've been arrested. You've gone to jail.

There is a history of civil disobedience in this country. You can go back to the movement against slavery, to Thoreau's protest against the Mexican war, to the abolitionists, white and black, who violated the Fugitive Slave Act of 1850 and rescued slaves from the police and from their masters. A long tradition in American history of people being willing to violate the law, commit civil disobedience in order to make a declaration of what is right and what is just. And people do that because they want to dramatize the principles of democracy. In the case of Thoreau going to jail, he wanted to dramatize the fact that the United States had just provoked a war with Mexico, a war of conquest.

The abolitionists who were freeing the slaves and violating the Fugitive Slave Act were trying to declare the principle that no man or woman should be enslaved by anybody else. And the people in the labor movement who were arrested again and again for acts of civil disobedience for violating laws that were designed to keep them down—they were trying to establish the principle that working people in this country should have rights, should not be subject to total domination by the employers they work for. And in the civil rights movement, in the antiwar movement of the 1960s, again, people committed acts of civil disobedience. And in the Vietnam War there were people who refused to be drafted, GIs who deserted. These were acts of civil disobedience. And all designed to make a powerful point.

That's what civil disobedience does: It makes a point more powerfully than a petition or statement or letter to your congressman. It's a way of dramatizing a principle that you want to uphold, dramatizing a grievance that you want to point to. So it has always been an important and necessary tactic in any social movement, and one that has at certain times in history been effective in arousing other people to a cause.

5

RESISTANCE AND THE ROLE OF ARTISTS

Cambridge, Massachusetts
February 6, 2004

You often bring up the role of artists in a time of war. Why?

The reason I do is because artists play a very special role in relation to social change. This came to me when I was a teenager and becoming politically interested for the first time. It was people in the arts who perhaps had the greatest emotional effect on me. Singers such as Pete Seeger, Woody Guthrie, and Paul Robeson. Writers like Upton Sinclair and Jack London. I was reading the newspapers and Karl Marx. I was reading all sorts of subversive matter. But there was something special about the effect of what artists did.

And by artists I mean not only singers and musicians but poets, novelists, people in the theater. It always seemed to me that there was a special power that artists had when they commented, either in their own work or outside their work, on what was going on in the world. There was a kind of force that they brought into the discussion that mere prose could not match. Part of it had to do with a passion and an emotion which comes with poetry, which comes with music, that comes with drama, which is rarely equaled in prose, even if it is beautiful prose. I was struck by that at an early age.

Later, I came to think about the relative power of people in charge of society and the powerlessness of most people who become the victims of the decision makers. I thought about the possibility of people without the ordinary attributes of power, that is, money and military equipment, resisting those who have a monopoly on that power, and I thought how can they possibly resist it? I thought art gave them a special impetus through its inspiration and through its emotional effect that couldn't be calculated. Social movements all through history have needed art in order to enhance what they do, in order to inspire people, in order to give them a vision, in order to bring them together, make them feel that they are part of a vibrant movement.

You quote the poet Shelley in A People's History. *There's an interesting intersection with the American labor movement, where workers at the turn of the twentieth century were organizing, but they were also reading to other workers to inform them, to impart literature to them.*

It's interesting how very often people who are not acquainted with the workplace, people who have not worked in factories or mills, think that working people are not interested in literature, that they don't read, that they are not part of the reading public. But it has always been true that working people had a life outside of their workplace. And outside of their workplace they would read, and they would become self-educated. Sometimes in their workplace they would take whatever opportunity they had to talk to one another, to read to one another. They would take whatever opportunity they had to draw upon the great voices in literature. And that's what I was referring to in *A People's History,* when I was talking about the struggles of garment workers in the early part of the twentieth century. I was referring to the fact that they would read poetry to one another. One worker in her memoir talked about how they would read Shelley's poem "The Mask of Anarchy" and quote those inspiring lines:

> Rise like lions after slumber
> In unvanquishable number!
> Shake your chains to earth, like dew
> Which in sleep had fallen on you—
> Ye are many; they are few!

What a remarkable affirmation of the power of people who seem to have no power. Ye are many, they are few. It has always seemed to me that poetry, music, literature, contribute very special power.

Shelley wrote "The Mask of Anarchy" after a massacre in Manchester, England, in 1819 when eleven peaceful demonstrators were killed and hundreds wounded. They were protesting against the deplorable economic conditions at the time. He also wrote one about hubris and the arrogance of great emperors in "Ozymandias," which is Greek for Ramses, the ancient pharaoh of Egypt. " 'My name is Ozymandias, King of Kings: / Look on my works, ye Mighty, and despair!' / Nothing beside remains. Round the decay / Of that colossal wreck, boundless and bare / The lone and level sands stretch far away."

I remember in school reading that poem, but a lot of its meaning was lost to us. I don't think the teacher drew the full meaning of that poem, the transient nature of power. Power is temporary; it comes into being and it goes out. Great monuments and great works that look as if they will stand forever decay and they fall. Shelley was certainly a very politically aware person and had a connection to some of the anarchists of that time, including William Godwin, whose daughter he was involved with. Shelley had a certain connection with the anarchist idea, and the anarchist idea is based on, for one thing, the ephemeral nature of power and the fact that if enough people assemble their meager resources, they can together overcome the most powerful force.

You like the work of Langston Hughes. He wrote a poem entitled "Columbia." What draws you to him?

Langston Hughes is one of my favorite poets, and I suppose that's why he got into trouble. Not because he was one of my favorite poets but because he wrote the kind of poetry that would get him in trouble with the establishment. I remember he wrote a very short poem once called "Good Morning Revolution." But this particular poem you are referring to I chose because I see it as a forerunner, decades earlier, of Martin Luther King's speaking out against the Vietnam War. Hughes is speaking out here against the hubris of the United States as a new imperial power in the world. He's very skeptical of the claims of the United States to innocence in its forays in the world. He addresses the United States in this poem, saying, "My dear girl, / You haven't been a virgin so long." And goes on to say that the United States is "one of the world's big vampires." So, he asks:

> *Why don't you come on out and say so*
> *Like Japan, and England, and France,*
> *And all the other nymphomaniacs of power. . . .*

Langston Hughes also leads me to think of Zora Neale Hurston. Zora Neale Hurston was a magnificent African American writer.

Very southern and unclassifiable. Nobody could put her in any kind of slot and categorize her. Very often she offended other black people by the things she would say. She was a totally honest person; she just spoke her mind. She wasn't afraid of going against the conventional so-called wisdom of the day. So when World War II broke out and everyone was supposed to jump on the bandwagon and support the war, Zora Neale Hurston would not go along with that. She saw the war as not simply a war between democratic, liberty-loving nations against fascist nations; she saw it as a war of one set of empires against another set of empires. She wrote her autobiography in 1942, shortly after Pearl Harbor. In *Dust Tracks on a Road* she said that she could not get teary-eyed, as everyone was doing, over what the Japanese and Germans were doing to their subject peoples. It's not that she was supporting what they were doing or that she approved of what they were doing. But she said they're doing what the Western powers, now supposedly on the good side of the war, are doing. They're doing what the Dutch have done in Indonesia, what the English have done in India, what the Americans have done in the Philippines. They are doing the same thing. Her publisher cut that out of her autobiography. It wasn't put back until many, many years after World War II when a new edition of *Dust Tracks on a Road* came out. When the United States bombed Hiroshima and destroyed several hundred thousand human beings, Zora Neale Hurston wrote about Truman as the Butcher of Asia. Nobody else was speaking that way about Harry Truman.

But I bring her up because of this tradition of black writers, poets, intellectuals going beyond the issue of race. Of course, not totally beyond because they are watching people of color around the world being brutalized by the white imperial nations of the world, but going beyond the racial question in the United States to talk about what happens to people in other parts of the world.

Let's jump a little chronologically to Bob Dylan and his "Masters of War."

Dylan is the great folksinger of the sixties, of the civil rights movement, of the movement against the war in Vietnam. There is probably no voice, no music more powerful than his in expressing the indignation of that generation against racism and against war. He was a genius with words and with music, speaking with such power that his words echo today. Not only do they echo today in relation to what happened then, but they echo because they are so relevant to today.

I chose to quote "Masters of War" because I thought, well, of course, he was talking about that time, and about the Vietnam War, but he could just as well be talking about the wars we have fought since Vietnam, and particularly the war of today, of the United States against Iraq. "Masters of War" is still being sung, not just by Dylan but by many other singers. I was at a concert not long ago here in Boston and heard Eddie Vedder of Pearl Jam sing "Masters of War." The huge and appreciative audience consisted mostly of young people. Pearl Jam is one of the most popular musical groups in the country. Eddie Vedder and Pearl Jam are bringing the Dylan sensibility to a whole new generation. Dylan's song must be heard to convey the full measure of its power, but I will spare you by not singing it. All I can do is faintly suggest its impact. He addresses himself to "You that build big guns, / You that build the death planes. . . ." He says to them that they play with the world as if it's their little toy. And he asks the "Masters of War": "Is your money that good? / Will it buy you forgivness, do you think that it could?"

Another artist who has achieved widespread popularity is filmmaker and writer Michael Moore. He's had several bestselling books. At the Seventy-fifth Academy Awards ceremony in March 2003, he received the Oscar for his documentary Bowling for Columbine, *and with a global audience of perhaps a billion people watching he said "Shame on you, Mr. Bush," and he denounced the war. A bit later the Spanish filmmaker Pedro Almodovar also made a very strong antiwar statement, albeit a little low-key.*

I think it's admirable when artists use an occasion to do what they're not supposed to do, that is, speak out on what's going on in the world. They are just supposed to immerse themselves in the spectacle of the moment, of the Oscars, of this Hollywood extravaganza. They are supposed to shut out the world and just feast on the glitter of what people are wearing and what trophies people are taking away. It is impolite and unprofessional to say that people are dying in other parts of the world while we are sitting here in our resplendent dress and giving out and receiving prizes. I admire the people who break out of the rule that you must be silent and be what they call a professional.

This rule of not going outside the boundaries is a rule that is welcomed very strongly by people in power. They want all of us to stay within the boundaries set by our professions. I have faced this myself as a historian. As a historian, I am supposed to just do history, and if I show up at the meeting of the American Historical Association in 1969 and propose a resolution that the historians should speak out against the war in Vietnam, well there's shock.

We're historians; we're supposed to be here to talk about history and present our papers and leave matters of life and death to politicians. Rousseau had something to say about that. Back in the late eighteenth century, Rousseau said we have all sorts of specialties—we have engineers, we have scientists, we have ministers—but we no longer have a citizen among us. Somebody who will go beyond our professional prison and take part in the combat for social justice.

The people who break out of that, like Michael Moore, I think deserve an enormous amount of credit. You talk about Michael Moore being able to reach a huge number of people. People in the entertainment world have a possibility of reaching larger numbers of people than we do, and if they miss out on an opportunity to reach huge numbers of people, then they are depriving all of us of the very special opportunity.

So the Dixie Chicks speak out, as they did, using words similar to Michael Moore. One of the Dixie Chicks said I am ashamed that I come from Texas, which is George Bush's state. This was a wonderful thing to do.

One of the valuable things about big stars speaking out is that they may be condemned for speaking out on social issues, but their talents are powerful enough to overcome that. People don't stop going to their concerts. People didn't stop going to hear the Dixie Chicks. And people didn't stop reading Michael Moore's books; in fact, they sold even more after that event. And people aren't going to stop seeing Jessica Lange's movies. I think all these opportunities should be seized.

A friend of mine who was in Spain wrote to me. He pointed out that in the American Academy Awards, it was only a rare person like Michael Moore who would speak out and declare his political views. But in Europe that's accepted. The Spanish equivalent of the Oscars are called Goyas. That is interesting in itself, since Goya is the great antiwar painter, depicting the horrors of the Napoleonic wars. This friend was telling me that the recipients of the Goyas in Spain, almost every single one of them that year at the beginning of Bush's war on terrorism, almost every single one of them who got up to the microphone wore an antiwar button or banner on their clothes.

Molly Ivins, the syndicated columnist and author of the bestseller Bushwhacked, *reports on citizens who say they are not interested in politics and have this sense of resignation and hopelessness. What do you say to people who feel there is no use in getting involved?*

Well, like Molly Ivins, I hear those cynical comments a lot. It's interesting because I may be speaking to a college audience or an audience of community people, fifteen hundred people, and someone gets up from the audience and says, What can I do? We're really helpless. And I say, Look around. There are fifteen hundred people sitting here. These fifteen hundred people have just applauded me very enthusiastically for speaking out against the war or for speaking out against the monopolization of power and wealth. That's just in this small community. There are fifteen hundred people or two thousand people everywhere in the United States who feel the way you do, who feel the way I do, and in fact not only are they feeling that way but more and more of them are acting on behalf of their feelings. Very often you don't know what they are doing because in the United States we are so fragmented. It is a very big country. The media do not report what is happening in other parts of the country. You may not even know what's happening in your part of the country. Maybe you may know what's happening in your neighborhood but not even in another part of your city, the newspapers, the media, do not report the activities of ordinary people. They will report what the president ate yesterday, but they will not report the gathering of a thousand or two thousand people on behalf of some important issue. So keep in mind that all over this country there are many, many people who add up to the millions of people who care about the same things you do.

Now whether their caring can have an effect is something you can't judge immediately. Here is where history comes in handy. If you look back at the development of social movements in history, what do you find? You find that they start with hopelessness. They start with small groups of people meeting, acting in their local communities and looking at the enormous power of the government or the enormous power of corporations and thinking, we don't have a chance—there is nothing we can do. And then what you find at certain points of history is that these small movements become larger ones, they grow, they grow. There's a kind of electronic vibration that moves across from one to the other. This is what happened in the sit-in movements in the sixties. This is how the civil rights movement developed. It developed out of the smallest of actions taken in little communities—in Greensboro, North Carolina, or Albany, Georgia—and moved and moved and grew until it became a force that the national government had to recognize. And we've seen this again and again. So at any early point in the development of a movement, things look hopeless, and if you are so intimidated by this hopelessness that you don't act, then those small groups will never become large ones.

John Lewis on the fortieth anniversary of the March on Washington reminded people that they were able to do that without the Internet, without cell phones, without faxes, just simply going door-to-door and phones calls. And there were no answering machines in those days. If you didn't get someone, there was no way to leave a message. But they were able to organize an enormous event.

That's an interesting point that John Lewis made because we tend to think now that what we have now is indispensable. My God, what did people do? I mean, how could Tolstoy write without a computer? But human beings have enormous capabilities. It's the nature of human beings to be ingenious and inventive. To figure out means of communication. To learn how to take whatever advantage they have, whatever small openings there are in a controlled system, and reach out to one another and communicate with one another. And so, yes, the civil rights movement grew as a result of people doing the most elemental things, of going into little towns and going door-to-door and holding meetings in churches and talking to people. During the Vietnam War people set up community newspapers and underground newspapers and organized teach-ins and rallies and GI coffeehouses. GIs could come and meet with one another and share antiwar views and be encouraged by learning that there were other GIs who felt the same way. So social movements have always been able to overcome the limits of communication. Now that we have the Internet, we have more tools at our command.

In a recent column in The Progressive, *you write that "We are at a turning point in the history of the nation . . . and the choice will come in the ballot box."*

I'm a little embarrassed that I said it, since it is always said. Everyone thinks they are at a turning point in history. But I actually believe that today, in the United States, we are at a special turning point. We have an administration in power that is more ruthless, more tied to corporate power, more militaristic, more ambitious in its desire to seize control and influence in all parts of the world, even in space, to militarize space. We have an administration that I believe is more dangerous than any administration we've ever had in American history. It has the capacity to send its armed forces all over the world, to kill large numbers of people; it has the capacity to use nuclear weapons. And these are people who seem unconstrained by the democratic idea that they should listen to other voices. It's an administration that won 47 percent of the popular vote in the last election, was put into office by a 5-to-4 vote of the Supreme Court in a very shady and tainted election. It immediately seized 100 percent of the power and began to use that power to control the wealth of the country and to assert military power abroad. We have a government that has so far been unrestrained in its use of power. It feels that there are no countervailing forces, that the United States, with ten thousand nuclear weapons, with more than a hundred military bases all over the world, is in a position to do whatever it wants. This makes this a very special time. And the reason I said so much hinges on the next election—and this is an unusual statement for me because I rarely think that that much hinges on elections—is that I believe we need to defeat George Bush in the next election because this is an especially cruel and ruthless administration. To beat George Bush should be a very high priority, an indispensable priority for anybody who wants to see a different kind of country. I don't think that electing another person other than George Bush is going to really solve the fundamental problems that we have because our experience has been that both Democratic and Republican administrations have been aggressive in foreign policy and have been tied to corporate power and corporate interests. But I think that another president coming into power after George Bush, a president who necessarily comes into power distinguishing himself from the policies of George Bush and criticizing the policies of George Bush, will be in a position where he has to in some sense answer to his constituency. And the constituency that will elect the next president, other than George Bush, will be a constituency that is antiwar and wants to change the priorities of the country from using the enormous wealth of the country for a military budget and tax breaks for corporations to using the great wealth for the needs of ordinary people.

We live in a country where in some places it is easier to buy a gun than to vote. Why are elections on Tuesday, a workday? Why not have them on the weekend? And why do we have a winner-take-all electoral college system rather than one-person–one-vote majority rule?

Those are very good questions. Why do we have the election on Tuesday when working people are at work? Executives of corporations and big business people can take time out any time they want. It's no surprise then that 50 percent of Americans don't vote in a presidential election. And many of them are working people. Many of them probably do find it hard to get away from their jobs on a Tuesday and go to vote.

Why don't we have one person one vote? Why do we have this absurd system of the electoral college? It was something that was set up in the eighteenth century, and we are still using it in the twenty-first century. One reason we have the system is that it is easily manipulated by powerful political groups, and it creates the possibility that very small manipulation of votes can win all of the electoral votes in a state. By doing enough chicanery to move your vote from

49.9 percent to 50.1 percent, you then get 100 percent of the state's electoral votes. It is a system that lends itself to corruption.

We saw this most blatantly in the 2000 presidential election. By giving Bush, in a very shady way, a 500-vote plurality, he got all of the electoral votes of Florida, enough to give him, in the eyes of the Supreme Court, the presidency. So we do not have a very democratic system. We have a democratic system when you compare it to totalitarian systems. We have a democratic system when you compare it to dictatorships, where you don't have elections. But we would be deceiving ourselves if we thought that because we don't have a totalitarian system and because we don't have a military dictatorship that therefore we have a democracy, that we have free elections. It's hypocritical of the United States to demand very haughtily that other countries should have free elections and then we will declare them democracies, when we ourselves have elections that are not free.

They are not free in the sense that money is involved. Money dominates our election process. Huge sums of money are expended for one candidate or another. Both candidates, Democrats and Republicans, need to amass enormous sums of money in order to win. Those sums of money do not come from ordinary people. They come from the big business interests. So it's not a free election in that sense.

And it's not a free election in the sense that people have the freedom to choose whatever candidate they want because the Democratic and Republican parties dominate the entire system. Third parties don't have an opportunity. If you have a presidential debate on television, third party candidates are not allowed to appear. All the people see are the Democratic and Republican parties. It's hardly a free choice. It is a very limited choice that people have.

Another aspect is that citizens who commit crimes and serve the time come out and then are denied the right to vote for the rest of their lives.

One of the really scandalous things that happened in the 2000 election in Florida is that they went through the rolls, and where they found people who had criminal records, they removed them from the voting rolls. Many thousands were removed. Since the people in the prisons in the United States are disproportionately people of color, it was people of color who were denied to right to vote.

Going back to literature, talk about Graham Greene's Quiet American, which was also made into a film. Why do you like Greene's novel?

It's refreshing to find a novelist who doesn't simply concentrate, as so many contemporary novelists do today, on the relationship of two people, three people, or four people. It's refreshing to find a novelist who looks outside of them and sees what the larger society is doing and gives the reader a kind of social consciousness, who does something more than say something about the romantic involvement of these two or three or four people. We have so many novels these days that simply deal in a very microscopic way with what is called relationships. You wouldn't know that there is anything else going on in the world.

I think the really important novels deal with personal stories, but they also put these personal stories in a social context, like *The Grapes of Wrath* and *Native Son*. *The Quiet American* is a very personal story. It has the anguish of a love story, a triangle of people are involved, an American, a British, a Vietnamese woman, but it is a story that goes beyond that. The setting is Vietnam, and it is the time when the United States is getting involved in Vietnam in a very insidious way. *The Quiet American* refers to an American who appears innocent but who really is working secretly for the American government. In the guise of stopping communism, he is engaging in atrocious acts that kill men, women, and children in Saigon. This is the social setting for this personal story of love.

It's interesting that when this film was recently released, Miramax, a giant in the film industry, held it back and was afraid to release it because it would be considered unpatriotic. It's unpatriotic to suggest that the United States in its policy in Vietnam was doing something immoral. Commentary and criticism on the morality of government policy is considered outside the pale, this in a supposedly democratic country. So they held the film for a while. It took the influence and power of its star, Michael Caine, brought to bear on Miramax, that finally caused the film's release. However, I noticed that it has not been given an enormous amount of attention or advertising as other films have. It's been consigned to a certain small number of theaters in the country. They've tried to limit the audience for a film that would dare to make a statement about the United States.

Dalton Trumbo wrote Johnny Got His Gun. *He was blacklisted and went to jail in the McCarthy era. He couldn't find work under his own name for years. Why did you assign this book to students?*

I chose the book because I've always believed that a work of art can bring a point home better than any prosaic exposition. I could give ten lectures about war and give them in such a way as to express my passionate feelings against war, and they would not have the impact that a student reading *Johnny Got His Gun* for one evening would feel.

Dalton Trumbo took the cruelty of war to the most extreme point: to take a soldier who is found on the battlefield barely alive but without arms, without legs, blind, deaf, the senses gone, really just a torso with the heart beating and a brain. This thing, this strange human being is picked up from the battlefield and brought into a hospital and put on a cot. The book consists of this person's brain operating and thinking.

There are two stories going on simultaneously. One is the thinking of this human being. All he can do is think: think about his past, his life, his small town, his girlfriend, the mayor of the town sending him off with great ceremony, going off to fight for democracy and liberty. He brings this all back and thinks about all of this.

At the same time, in the hospital ward he is trying to figure out how to communicate with the outside world. He can't speak. He can't hear. He can only sense vibrations. He can sense sunlight. He can feel the warmth of the sun and the cool of the evening. That's a way he can build up a calendar in his mind. He figures out a way of communicating with a nurse who is empathetic and ingenious enough to figure out what he is trying to do by using his head to tap against a piece of furniture. He taps out messages in code and the nurse deciphers them, and they communicate that way.

The climax comes when the big brass comes in to give him a medal. Through this nurse, they ask him, what do you want? And he thinks, what do I want? He taps out his response. The response, in the language of this generation, blows you away. He tells them what he wants. What he wants they cannot give him, of course. They cannot give him his arms, his legs, his sight. He asks them to take him into the school houses, classrooms, churches, wherever there are people, where there are young kids. He says, point to me and say, this is war. Their response is, this is beyond regulations. That's their answer. They want him to be forgotten.

This is a metaphor for our time. They want us to forget about the GIs. They want to forget about the guys who come back from war with legs gone, with arms gone, or blinded. No one may be as total a catastrophe as the character in *Johnny Got His Gun*, but there are people who in one way or another represent what he represents: the horrors of war.

But the government—we see this with the Bush administration—does not want people to be conscious of the fact that there are thousands and thousands of veterans of this war in Iraq who have come back blinded or without limbs. They've completely hidden that fact from the public. Only occasionally does a glimpse of that come through. There was a story in the *New York Times* not long ago about a GI who was blinded in Iraq. He was a young guy who was hit by shell fragments. His mother visits him in the hospital. When she visits him, she passes the cots of other young people without arms, without legs. She sees a young woman soldier who is back from Iraq without legs, crawling on the floor with her little child crawling behind her. This is the picture that the present administration wants to hide from the American people. A novel like *Johnny Got His Gun* can awaken its readers to an understanding of what war is like and how the government wants to hide the reality of war, the reality of what happens to our people, and certainly of what happens to people on the other side.

6

CRITICAL THINKING

Cambridge, Massachusetts
July 21, 2004

The year 2004 saw a number of anniversaries, most particularly the sixtieth anniversary of D-Day. But there was another event that went under the media radar, and that was FDR's 1944 State of the Union address on economic justice, where he laid out a rather radical vision of what American society could be like. He spoke of "the right to a useful and remunerative job. . . . the right to earn enough to provide adequate food and clothing and recreation. . . . the right of every family to a decent home; the right to adequate medical care and the opportunity to achieve and enjoy good health; the right to adequate protection from the economic fears of old age, sickness, accident, and unemployment; the right to a good education."

That is a forgotten moment in the presidency of FDR, when he outlined an Economic Bill of Rights. It is still sort of a surprise to Americans, who know that we have a Bill of Rights, to be told that this Bill of Rights applies only to certain political rights, such as the right to free speech and assembly, the right to a lawyer, the right to a fair trial. People are surprised when you tell them, "But, you know, the Bill of Rights does not include economic rights, does not include the right to health care, does not include the right to a job, does not include the right to decent housing, does not include the right to food." And without these rights, without economic rights, how can people make use of the political rights? Because, after all, what good is freedom of speech if you don't have the wherewithal to utilize that freedom? What good is the right to counsel if you can't afford to get a lawyer, and therefore you must have a court-appointed lawyer? All of the political rights are subject to the weakness that if there is no Economic Bill of Rights, then they don't have very much meaning.

Roosevelt, in 1944, was in the midst of World War II. Wars bring out the best of rhetoric because it is necessary to mobilize an entire population for war. And the best way to do that is to tell them what the future holds in store for them and to envision a grand future where their problems will be solved. And so, yes, 1944 was the right time for FDR to present his Economic Bill of Rights.

Interestingly enough, the provisions of the Economic Bill of Rights were then incorporated in the United Nations in the Universal Declaration of Human Rights. Eleanor Roosevelt was a bridge between FDR and the UN. She helped get it adopted. And this Universal Declaration of Human Rights includes all those provisions that FDR talked about: the right to remunerative employment, the right to health care, he right to education, the right to housing.

Both of those documents, it's fair to say, have been forgotten. FDR's Economic Bill of Rights has been pushed aside, ignored. I would guess that 95 percent of the American people do not know of its existence. And I would also guess that a similar percentage of the American people really don't know about the UN Universal Declaration of Human Rights. But it's important to remind people of them, because those are legitimate, important goals for American society and for world society today.

Robert Kuttner, in today's Boston Globe, *writes, "More workers have lost health insurance and pension coverage" in this period and that "these policy changes did not just happen, they were worked out in concert with organized business."*

It's been a long story, that the major parties are closely tied to big business, to corporate power. Corporate power does not support the idea of health care for everybody; they support privatization of the medical system. At this moment, because the Republican Party has been in power, there is a tendency to say, "You see what happened under the Bush administration: more people have lost their health care." The fact is, this was also happening under a Democratic administration. Both the Democrats and the Republicans have ignored the necessity of free, universal health care for everyone.

Going back to FDR for a moment: He innovated this idea of Fireside Chats, talking to the American people and using this new electronic medium—which was becoming widespread at that time—the radio. What was it like listening to him on the radio?

The Fireside Chat was a remarkable innovation. People all over the country sat around the radio and listened to Roosevelt's broadcasts. They were not like the canned speeches that we have heard from presidents since then, and they really did have the atmosphere of a fireside chat. Roosevelt himself was a great communicator. He could speak to people without a teleprompter, and he could make people feel that, yes, he was speaking very personally to them. We have not had the likes of such communication since then.

Even though he was from a wealthy patrician family.

It's certainly clear historically that you cannot tell the policies of the president by whether the president has a patrician background, like Roosevelt, or perhaps a middle-class or lower-class background, like Reagan, because once somebody has been catapulted into political power, into the White House, that class background becomes unimportant. What really becomes important are the pressures and forces circulating around the White House. What really becomes important is what's happening in the nation.

And what was happening in the nation when FDR was president was that, whatever his background—yes, rich, aristocratic—he had to listen to what was going on. And what was going on in the nation was that a country was in the midst of turmoil, a country that was suffering deeply from the Depression, and people were reacting against this militantly, with strikes all over the country. There were general strikes in San Francisco and Minneapolis, a huge textile strike in the South, with people organizing, tenants organizing, unemployed organizing, and a kind of danger to the system by the growth of radicalism in the 1930s. Roosevelt was responding to this. His patrician background didn't matter. Reagan, when he became president, did not have that kind of situation in the country, and Reagan was surrounded by big business and corporations and acted accordingly.

Did FDR save capitalism?

I think it's reasonable to say that FDR saved capitalism. After all, he did not want capitalism to go down the drain, and capitalism did look in danger in the 1930s. It was a time ripe for radical thought about radical change. Socialists and Communists and radicals of all sorts were in their heyday in the 1930s because people were looking for radical solutions and people were wondering whether capitalism was really the way to take care of people's needs. So Roosevelt acted, you might say, in the best interests of the capitalist class because he did the kinds of things that would mollify radicals, that would mollify people who might become radicals, by persuading them that capitalism can have a human face: Capitalism can give you Social Security, can give you unemployment insurance, can give you subsidized housing. So, yes, in a very important sense, he did save capitalism.

After the peak of unemployment in the early 1930s, by 1939, 1940, and 1941, unemployment was going up again. And then the war came. Some say the war bailed FDR out because it alleviated the unemployment problem.

It's true. While Roosevelt's measures took the worst edges off the Depression and ameliorated the problem of unemployment to a certain extent, it did not solve the problem of unemployment; it did not solve the problem of poverty. Even the measures—Social Security, for instance—gave very meager amounts of money to people when they retired. Unemployment insurance didn't match the unemployment insurance provisions, for instance, to be found in other Western European countries. The minimum wage that was passed was a minimum wage that started with twenty-five cents an hour and was to go up to forty cents an hour. So, poverty still existed, homelessness; the need for housing still existed, even after the New Deal reforms had done all that they could.

And, yes, the war created the absolute necessity for people to be given jobs because so much production was needed to send the materials to the front. It's a sad commentary on the capitalist system that the capitalist system could solve unemployment only through war. But, in fact, it's sort of a basic fact about this system that it is driven to give people jobs only when those jobs contribute to war and militarism. And there is such a thing as military Keynesianism. Keynesianism is the idea that, yes, the government should do something to interfere with the economy and regulate the economy in such a way as to help people at the bottom. Military Keynesianism is even more effective than ordinary Keynesianism because there is the profit motive for corporations operating to give people jobs in war industries. It's a commentary on the capitalist system that that seems to be the only way it can maintain economic stability.

Let's see how those threads of the system continue today, where the United States has an empire of bases. It's fighting two wars—one in Afghanistan and one in Iraq—and it's said that a lot of the volunteers are economically driven to join the military.

This has always been true, even when there was a draft. For people at the lower end of the economic spectrum, people who grow up in families where there is no money, people with little education, people who drop out of high school, or even graduate from high school and find there are no jobs for them, there is the lure of the military, promising them steady work and promising them health care. In the military there is no such thing as having to buy health insurance. When you're in the military, there is free, universal health care. And then, there is the promise that when you finish your military service, you will get educational benefits, something like the GI Bill of Rights, which was enacted for World War II veterans. So there are great economic incentives to young people from poor families to join the military.

Generally, when they join the military, they don't envision going into war and dying or killing. Then they are surprised and shocked by what they suddenly encounter—that they have, in effect, offered their lives or their limbs for economic security.

Jessica Lynch was from a rural town in West Virginia and was, momentarily, a hero of the Iraq war, for much exaggerated reasons. She joined the military, apparently, after she could not get a part-time job in the local Wal-Mart in her West Virginia town.

Jessica Lynch is just typical of a large, large percentage of the people who join the military. And so war is a class phenomenon. It is the poor who go to war, who get wounded and die in war.

In A People's History *you quote Randolph Bourne, "War is the health of the state."*

Randolph Bourne wrote that around the time of World War I. He saw that war was something that the state needs, that the government needs, for various reasons but one of them being that it gives the government a reason for existence. It gives the government a rationale for all it does. It gives the government more security from the possible rebelliousness of its own population when they face difficult conditions. Because war gives the government, the state, as Randolph Bourne put it, an opportunity to unite the country around a foreign enemy and therefore to put into the shadows the grievances that people have against their own system.

Talk more about economic justice. Bernie Sanders is the lone independent in the House of Representatives. In an article he writes, "There has always been a wealthy elite and there has always been a gap between the rich and the poor. But the current disparities in wealth and

income haven't been seen in over a hundred years. Today, the richest
1 percent own more wealth than the bottom 95 percent, and the CEOs
of large corporations earn more than five hundred times what their av-
erage employees make."

Bernie Sanders is certainly giving us an accurate picture of the situation. We've always, as he says, had this great disparity between rich
and poor; we've always had a class society. I've looked at the records
in the Colonies just before and just after the American Revolution,
and what they show is that around that time, 1 percent of the population owned 33 percent of the wealth. You could take that figure all
through American history, and it will deviate maybe only five or six
or seven percentage points one way or the other. Today, the figure is
not 1 percent owning 33 percent, but 1 percent owning 40 or 41 percent. But that disparity has always existed. Even before the ratio of
CEO salaries to ordinary worker salaries became 500 to 1, it was 40
or 50 to 1, which is bad enough. But it's true that in recent years—
and not just with the accession of the Republican Bush but through
the Clinton period—the ratio has kept changing drastically in the
direction of huge, huge sums of money to the heads and managers
of corporations.

Is this unique to the United States?

In general, in what they call free-market societies, capitalist
societies—*free market* being a euphemism, a nice polite term that
they like to use so that we don't have to use this terrible left-wing
term *capitalism*—there is this huge gap between rich and poor.
Here we have an example, in the former Soviet Union, where, whatever you can say about Stalinism—and you can say a lot of terrible
things accurately about Stalinism—while there was a kind of

privileged elite connected with the Communist Party, you did not have businessmen making billions of dollars.

Today, after the Soviet Union has collapsed, American political leaders and other people in the business world have said very happily, "Well, now free enterprise will come to the Soviet Union, the market system." The market system in the Soviet Union has been disastrous. It has resulted in the flow of enormous wealth to a handful of people, while at the bottom there is great difficulty for people in surviving. I think this is just a general fact about the market system.

Life expectancy has dramatically declined in Russia and other parts of the former Soviet Union.

That's one of the very sad things. Under Soviet rule, while they had to endure the tyranny of Stalin, they did have a decent health system and guaranteed health care for everybody. And now, with privatization, life expectancy has gone down to startling levels.

Silvio Berlusconi is prime minister of Italy and also a major media mogul. He took umbrage when a comparison was made between Saddam Hussein and Mussolini. He said, "That was a much more benign dictatorship. Mussolini did not murder anyone. Mussolini sent people on holiday to internal exile."

One of the first important books that I read when I was growing up was a book about Mussolini's Italy. It was *Sawdust Caesar* by George Seldes, a remarkable American journalist. Seldes was a correspondent in Italy when Mussolini came to power, and he saw what Mussolini was doing. Mussolini never murdered anybody? Somebody should have mentioned to Berlusconi the name of Giacomo Matteotti. Matteotti was a member of the Italian parliament who, when

Mussolini came to power, dared to criticize him. Shortly after, Matteotti was dragged out of his house and murdered. There was no question about who murdered him.

As for sending people on vacation, maybe Berlusconi was sent on vacation. He's accustomed to nice vacations. The people that Mussolini sent abroad were soldiers sent to Ethiopia to kill Ethiopians in a war that was designed to sort of restore the glory of the Roman Empire. Fortunately, Berlusconi, despite his control of the press, has not been able to mesmerize the people of Italy, who, despite his control of the press, turned out in huge numbers to protest the present war in Iraq, which Berlusconi is supporting.

In terms of fascism in the United States, Sinclair Lewis wrote a novel in the mid-1930s, It Can't Happen Here. *About fifteen years later, Robert Penn Warren wrote* All the King's Men. *His character Willy Stark was loosely based on the charismatic and flamboyant Kingfish of Louisiana, Huey Long, who once said, "If fascism ever came to the United States, it would be wrapped in an American flag."*

I remember reading *It Can't Happen Here.* Interestingly enough, it's probably the least known of Sinclair Lewis's novels. He's probably best known for *Babbitt* and *Arrowsmith.* But as soon as a well-known novelist writes something political, then whatever he wrote is sort of pushed into obscurity. The same thing happened with Mark Twain, of course a famous novelist. But his political writings were sort of kept in obscurity. Sinclair Lewis wrote *It Can't Happen Here* in the 1930s, when fascism had arisen in Italy and Germany, and people were saying, "It can't happen here in the United States." He wrote a novel to show how it could happen in the United States.

There is, in my opinion, no clear-cut difference between a fascist state and other forms of government, other states, including a liberal, democratic, capitalist state like the United States. When I say no clear-cut difference, of course, there are differences, but it isn't a polar difference. It isn't as if you have fascism at one end of the spectrum and American democracy at the other end of the spectrum. I believe that in a country like the United States, which has certain democratic liberties and a certain degree of freedom of the press and a certain degree of freedom of speech, nevertheless there are aspects of American society that I would say resemble fascism.

I point to the prison system; I point to the two million people who are in the prison system in the United States. If somebody asked you, "Could you describe the prison conditions in Iraq?" the ones that have just been brought into the limelight, torture and horrible treatment of prisoners, well, prisoners in American prisons—and I receive letters to this effect because I have correspondence with American prisoners—have said, "Don't they realize that the same kinds of things happen in American prisons? That there are sadistic guards, sadistic wardens, that we are tortured? Don't they realize that people in police stations are tortured to get confessions from them?" As soon as you enter that area of American society, as soon as you go into the police station and then into the jail, then into the prison, you have removed yourself from the Bill of Rights. From that point on, you are a helpless victim of whatever the authorities want to do to you. And I would argue that that's a form of fascism.

The main character in It Can't Happen Here *is a newspaper editor, Doremus Jessup. Toward the end of the novel, when he's in jail, he says, "The tyranny of this dictatorship isn't primarily the fault of big business nor of the demagogues who do their dirty work. It's the fault*

of Doremus Jessup, of all the conscientious, respectable, lazy-minded
Doremus Jessups who have let the demagogues wriggle in without
fierce enough protest."

That's a very interesting passage. Jessup understood something that
would be important for us to understand today—that if fascism did
come to the United States, it would come as a result of the silence
and the pitiful weakness of the American media, who would, as
they have done again and again, go along with whatever the president says so long as he says he is doing it for national security.

This is exactly what has been happening in the war in Iraq. If
you want to blame Bush and Cheney and the people in the White
House for getting us into an illegal and immoral war in Iraq, you
would also have to blame the press for going along with that, for not
raising an outcry. Because if the press, if television, which most
people watch, had raised an outcry about this, they would not be
able to get away with this war.

U.S. politicians are fond of quoting the Founding Fathers. Of course,
these quotes are used very selectively and they pick out the ones that
buttress their position. But here's one from James Madison. It's in-
scribed outside the Library of Congress, "A popular government with-
out popular information, or means of acquiring it, is but a Prologue
to a Farce or a Tragedy, or perhaps both. Knowledge will forever gov-
ern ignorance, and a people who mean to be their own governors
must arm themselves with the power which knowledge gives."

Madison's comment states a very important truth: Democracy is
meaningless if the public cannot get accurate information. If information is withheld from the public by government secrecy, the
public is misled by government lies, if the media do not report these

lies, and if the media do not investigate what the government is doing and watch very carefully what the government is doing, then we do not have a democracy. It's very nice that that's inscribed so that people in Washington can see it. I doubt that they read it.

Do you think the journalists know what's actually going on and choose not to report, or they're simply ignorant?

It's a complicated situation. There are all kinds of journalists. I think there are journalists who become wrapped up in nationalism and patriotism. And if they're given uniforms and told, "We will embed you in the American army"—I guess they could put it another way, that you will go to bed with the American army—"then you will have certain privileges." There are journalists, who, when they're offered that are just delighted. And then they are caught up in the atmosphere of the military and of winning and so on. How can they possibly report in an honest way what is going on?

And there are other journalists who will go outside of the official boundaries, just as some journalists in Vietnam, instead of just listening to the press accounts in Saigon, what were called the five o'clock follies in Saigon—every [day at] five o'clock the government would give them the truth—would venture out of that, and they would go out into the field and they would report on what was happening.

So there are some journalists in Iraq who have reported—and I've seen some, and there haven't been too many—accounts in mainstream newspapers of a reporter who goes into a hospital and goes to the bed of a ten-year-old kid who has lost an arm and a leg and is blinded by an American bombing and who reports on that. So there are different kinds of reporters.

But the higher up in the journalistic hierarchy, the more diffi-cult it is to really become independent. The editors are more con-servative than the reporters.

Is the system just so powerfully seductive?

The system has the power to give jobs to people and to offer people job security. You said I was in the knowledge industry. Journalists are in an industry. If you're in an industry, then you are part of a hierar-chy of power and influence. Your job, your security, whether you're a reporter or a college professor, is dependent on people above you who have more power than you do, so you have to be very careful about what you do so as not to displease them. So that operates in the culture of journalism.

And then, sometimes you have very blatant orders given down by the media moguls. I just saw an ad in the *New York Times* by MoveOn, in which they reported on the orders that are given by the Fox network executives to Fox reporters, saying things like, "Well, you know, you shouldn't really play up Iraqi civilian casu-alties."

I have a copy of that ad right here. It's dated July 20, 2004. "The Com-munists had Pravda, Republicans have Fox." One of the memos hand-ed down to the journalists said, "Let's refer to the U.S. marines we see in the foreground as 'sharpshooters,' not 'snipers,' which carries a nega-tive connotation."

Sharpshooters, not snipers. Snipers carries a negative connotation. And also, you could add to that list of language, the many thou-sands of people who have been hired by private corporations to be security people, really a paramilitary function in Iraq. The press has repeatedly referred to them as contractors, implying that they're just there for business reasons. The more accurate term would be mercenaries. They are being paid to work with the American military. They are armed; they're just not wearing uniforms. This is the privatization of an ugly war. So you can go on and on with the euphemisms that are used to describe this war.

You fought in World War II. Can you imagine a situation where perhaps the pilot of your bomber was a private contractor and not accountable to the so-called chain of command?

I think we would have rebelled at that time. Maybe we've gotten so accustomed to the idea of privatization that now we accept that. I must say that the idea of using a kind of language to disguise what is going on was happening in World War II also. We went on bombing missions. It's interesting, the word *mission*. The word *mission*, like *missionary*, suggests something benign, something good that you're doing: you're on a goodwill mission, you're on a medical mission. It was a bombing mission. You're dropping bombs on people. They don't say, "You're going on a mission to kill anybody who lives in this city." No, it's a mission. And when they described how many missions you were on to decide how many medals you could get, they would say you flew so many missions. No hint of what these missions were doing to ordinary people on the ground.

Or to those engaging in them.

Or what they were doing to the minds of those engaging in them, getting people in the air force accustomed to dropping bombs, no matter who they killed.

Fast-forwarding to today, where there is torture in U.S.-run prisons of Iraq, Afghanistan, and Guantánamo, there is a Geneva convention on torture. There is no Geneva convention on abuse. And the most prestigious newspaper in the country, the New York Times, refuses to use the word torture. It's an interesting choice of words. They use the term abuse. So if I keep you up for three days and deprive you of food and keep the lights on, and every time you try to fall asleep I wake you up or throw hot or cold water on you, that's not torture, that's abuse.

The U.S. government also has lawyers working for it. It's been interesting listening when these stories came out of Iraq to definitions of torture. You could hear this on public television, and I mention public television because you would expect it to be more independent, more critical of government than commercial television. That, in fact, is not so. You turn on PBS and you see that they're giving a lot of time to a government lawyer or a lawyer who has worked for the government, in fact, a lawyer who has written memos for the government in which his job is to try to explain and justify torture by how the word is defined.

Of course, lawyers are good at this. They go into complicated and obscure definitions of the word *torture* so as to show that these horrible things that are being done in Iraq and elsewhere really cannot be called torture and therefore are not violations of international law. This is a monstrous use of legal education.

Martin Luther King Jr., in his historic 1967 Riverside Church speech in New York, said, "Even when pressed by the demands of inner truth, men do not easily assume the task of opposing their government's policy, especially in time of war." Why is that?

We've seen this historically again and again. It's not easy for people to immediately decide that their government is wrong. We grow up with a belief in government. It's not inborn; it's cultivated. You grow up in this country learning that your country is a democracy, everybody has the right to vote, we have a Bill of Rights, you pledge allegiance to the flag, you salute, you grow up learning that the heroes of the country's history are military heroes. And when the government speaks, your first impulse is to believe, yes, the government is right. After all, we elected the government. There is a kind of belief that if you elected the government, then everything is democratic and you can trust the government.

You're also brought up to believe that your interests and the government's are the same. You're not brought up to look at history and find that very often the interests of the government are not the same as the interests of the people, especially when it comes to war. So you grow up believing that your interests are the same. You grow up with language that suggests a common interest: You grow up with phrases like the *national interest, national defense, national security*, implying that the government's security, the government's defense are all your defense.

Add to that kind of obfuscation of reality the fact that when the government sets out to go to war, it is in control of the information, and it is in a position of being able to create an atmosphere in which we're doing the right thing. The enemy is evil. We're going to war for civilization. We're going to war because something was done to us. The battleship *Maine* is blown up in Havana harbor in 1898. American troops have been attacked on the Mexican border. This happened in 1846. They have fired the first shots in the Philippines. This happened in 1901. They've attacked our destroyers in the Gulf of Tonkin. This is what happened in 1964. And the American public has no idea what is going on, the American public has no way of checking up on what the government tells them, so the tendency is to just believe the government.

And the public is not helped by members of Congress. Congress is presumably there to check the excesses of the executive branch. That's what they mean when they talk about checks and balances and separation of powers. That's what Congress is supposed to do. But Congress doesn't do that in matters of foreign policy. Congress goes along with absolute obsequiousness to whatever the president does. So if Congress does that, and then the newspapers go along and the TV networks go along, then the public has no independent source of information from which to criticize or to suspect that something is being put over on them.

Is the role of education to inculcate in students critical thinking and a sense of skepticism?

The university traditionally is supposed to be a place for independent thought and a place that teaches critical thinking. But, in fact, that may apply to trivial things, like what was the first capital of the United States or let's check up if they've given us the wrong date for the Boston Massacre. There is no problem in thinking critically when it comes to unimportant facts. But when it comes to really critical matters of life and death, of war and peace, you do not find that the educational system prepares young people to be critical of American foreign policy. You can go through the courses that are given all through the American educational system, and you will find very orthodox thinking.

You go into the departments of political science in universities, and you will see that the education that students get is Machiavellian.

By Machiavellian I mean that it's education from the point of view of the state. You will get courses in war games, you will get courses in public policy, always from the point of view of the government, what policy the government should pursue, and you will not really learn in a critical way about the history of American foreign policy.

In fact, the term for the study of American foreign policy in the scholarly world is *diplomatic history*. That's what it's called. And that's exactly what it is: It's diplomatic history; it's soft history. It's history in which the United States is generally a benign power, which may have occasional moments when it veers off from its customary position of being a decent country. But, in general, the education that young people get mostly does not prepare them to be critical thinkers about American society.

A constant criticism that is leveled against the left in this country is that we talk among ourselves; we preach to the choir. What do you think about that?

The choir and the congregation. It's probably true that often, maybe most of the time, people on the left speak to the choir. By the way, there is value in that. There is value in people speaking to people who already agree with them but who don't act on the principles that they believe in. And one of the reasons you have rallies and demonstrations—and you know that the people who are going to come to those rallies and demonstrations are people that already agree with the thrust of those demonstrations—is the idea of bringing the choir together to encourage people, inspire people, activate, motivate people. So it's not a terrible thing to preach to the choir.

However, it's not true that people on the left, critics of the American government speak only to people who agree with them. It's obviously not true. I'm thinking right now, at this moment in American history of Michael Moore's remarkable film, *Fahrenheit 9/11*, which, if it is speaking to the choir, is speaking to an enormous choir, obviously, speaking to millions of Americans who have never before experienced a left-wing rally or demonstration.

There are ways and times in which people on the left and left-wing ideas break through into the general population, into the mass media—break in maybe only temporarily and maybe only partially, but they do. Barbara Ehrenreich, for instance, is a person on the left. She's had a number of important columns in the *New York Times*. We've mentioned that her book *Nickel and Dimed* has sold in huge numbers. Documentary films are being shown to large audiences all over the country. Those of us who go around the country speaking— I'm talking about myself, Noam Chomsky, and others—don't speak only to little groups of radicals who come to listen to us.

I've spoken to fifteen hundred people in Morehead, Kentucky. There are not fifteen hundred radicals in Morehead, Kentucky. If there were fifteen hundred radicals in Morehead, then we would be on the verge of revolution. But no. Maybe there were fifty, and the other people came out of curiosity or because they were reading my book, *A People's History of the United States*, which, by the way, itself is an example of a piece of radical literature reaching out beyond the usual radical reading public.

I go to Athens, Georgia, and speak to eight hundred people. I remember Athens, Georgia, the seat of the Confederacy, when I was living in Atlanta. It was one of the most right-wing, reactionary places in the country. You would never dream that eight hundred people would show up to listen to a very sharp critique, as I like to characterize my talks, on the war. There is a radical columnist in the main newspaper of Athens. This is what I mean. There are radical voices breaking into the mainstream. So we are not talking only to the choir. I've spoken in Lincoln, Nebraska, in Springfield, Missouri, all sorts of odd places where large numbers of people turn out. Noam Chomsky speaks to huge crowds wherever he goes, and they're not just members of the choir.

Your former student at Spelman College, Alice Walker, wrote a book called Anything We Love Can Be Saved. *She writes that Malcolm X, Martin Luther King Jr., Fannie Lou Hamer, and Rosa Parks all "represent activism at its most contagious, because it is always linked to celebration and joy."*

That sounds like Alice Walker. She is a person who does not think that activism and critical thinking is a dour, sober, humorless enterprise. She believes that social movements are movements that generate a feeling, yes, of joy and excitement and of truly being alive. And I think that's a very important commentary that she makes, because I think it is important for people who maybe are wondering whether they should become involved in social movements and to work for peace and justice to know that this does not mean that they are going into a monastery but that they are going to be part of an enterprise which is joyful and fun and life-giving.

I'm afraid we're running out of time. I'm just going to end with one final question. And this is a very sensitive topic. I hope you don't take it badly.

I will.

I was wondering what you're planning to do when you get old. Have you been able to project that far ahead?

It's something actually that I don't think about because I've passed it. I've passed being old, and now I'm in some sort of special world where age doesn't count, where you don't think of it, where you just do what you have to do day after day. And it saves times and energy if you don't think about age or retirement or any of those dull words.

7

AIRBRUSHING HISTORY

Cambridge, Massachusetts
December 3, 2004

You just got back from Florida. You met with students at the elite Tampa Prep School. What did you talk about?

I went there because one of the students, who is quite political and progressive, and is only sixteen years old, wrote me a remarkably eloquent letter inviting me. I realized after I got there why she invited me. Because her classmates are, as she put it, the sons and daughters of the elite. The parents are Republicans. These are rich kids, and conservative. She wanted me to talk to them about the war, which I did. I spoke to an assembly of about two hundred. And because I had only a short time with them, I just spoke for about five minutes. I compressed my entire world philosophy and life into five minutes, just to give them an idea of where I stood. And then I threw it open, and we had a very lively back and forth. These kids were not shy, maybe because they come from families that give them confidence. Does money give you confidence? Maybe. In any case, it was lively because so many of them obviously disagreed with my position on the war, at least had questions about it.

But it was a good discussion because they asked the kinds of

questions that you might say ordinary Americans who have swal-
lowed the Bush line on the war would ask. But shouldn't we have
gotten rid of Saddam Hussein? Isn't it better that we got rid of Saddam Hussein? Isn't Iraq better off without Saddam Hussein? And be-
sides, what should we have done about September 11? Should we have
stood by? Should we have just sat and done nothing about September
11? And don't you believe in war, and don't you believe that war can
solve problems and settle things? And don't you think we need to
serve our country?

These are the kinds of questions I wanted. I love to talk about
those things. At the end of it, a lot of the students came up to me and
expressed their support for what I was saying. When you give a talk
like that, you don't know how much is going to sink in, you don't
know what effect you're going to have, you don't know if the students
will leave exactly as they entered. But my experience has been that
very often you drop thoughts into the minds of young people, and
they sort of germinate and something happens, not to all of them but
to some of them. So, all in all, it was a useful experience.

*Years ago you gave me tapes of a debate you had with William F.
Buckley at Tufts in January of 1971. I was listening to those tapes the
other day. I was interested to hear you say then that "The main thrust
of American foreign policy is toward war, toward armaments, toward
at this moment Vietnam, and tomorrow more adventures elsewhere in
the world."*

It wasn't very hard for me to predict that. For anybody who knew
anything about the history of American foreign policy, that person
would not expect that Vietnam would be the last imperial adven-
ture of the United States. Vietnam was just one in a very long suc-

cession of expansionist moves by the United States, starting with the conquest of the continent, the destruction of Indian tribes, and then moving into the Caribbean, and then moving across the Pacific at the turn of the century. So Vietnam was part of that long train of events. It wasn't hard for me or anybody else who knew American history to understand that what happened in Vietnam was likely to happen again.

There has been an arc of militarism, intervention, and imperialism. Talk about what is often described as the Age of Imperialism, the few short years during which the United States invaded the Philippines, Cuba, Guam, and other territories, and the uses of God in justifying the actions. In a chapter on this in A People's History, *"The Empire and the People," you quote McKinley saying, "I walked the floor of the White House night after night until midnight; and I'm not ashamed to tell you, gentlemen, that I went down on my knees and prayed Almighty God for light and guidance more than one night. And one night late it came to me this way." And then he goes on to list four reasons why the United States needed to invade the Philippines.*

McKinley invoked God to justify his decision to move the American army and navy into the Philippines. And one of the reasons he gave is we must civilize and Christianize the Filipinos, which was an interesting concept, considering that most Filipinos were Christian. But they apparently had a different view of what God's will was than McKinley did. They didn't think it was God's will for them to be conquered by the United States, so they fought back for a number of years. Your pointing out that there was something called the Age of Imperialism in American textbooks. Maybe it still is. And it usually refers to just a few years of American history, during which we took Cuba, the Philippines, Hawaii, Guam, the Virgin Islands, and Puerto Rico. And that takes care of the imperial history of the United States, according to most textbooks. But, of course, it had gone on for a long time before then and clearly has gone on for a long time since then.

Six decades after that burst of imperial violence, the United States was in Indochina, and today it is in Afghanistan and Iraq. Is it all part of that same trajectory?

I have no doubt about it. It's interesting, the way that propaganda works. It depends on amnesia. Amnesia suggests forgetting, but often in the case of the American people, it isn't that they have forgotten, it's that they never learned. So it's possible for an administration to give reasons for going into Iraq that are reasons of immediacy; that is, it's because there are weapons of mass destruction, it's because they're ruled by a tyrant, because they present a threat. And without any history, it's possible for people to believe that. But with some history it is not, then, hard to see the invasion of Iraq as part of that long chain of imperial adventures.

Edward Said wrote, "Part of the main plan of imperialism . . . is that we will give you your history, we will write it for you, we will reorder the past. . . . What's more truly frightening is the defacement, the mutilation, and ultimately the eradication of history in order to create . . . an order that is favorable to the United States."

The eradication of history. Certainly the history of the United States in relation to the Middle East has been eradicated as far as American culture is concerned. That is, very few Americans understand that this present war in Iraq goes back in its history to the very end of World War II; that is, it goes back for sixty years, goes back to that moment when in effect the United States was taking over control and domination of the Middle East from the British and French, who had taken control at the time of the First World War.

You see that interest in oil leaping into the forefront in 1953 in Iran. Mossadegh, a popular, elected, nationalist leader, nationalizes the oil fields. And that pronounces his doom, because that cannot be tolerated by the United States or other Western powers that are interested in oil. So the United States engineers a coup in Iran in 1953, a covert action, which now is quite well known, to overthrow Mossadegh and install the shah. Talk about the United States in favor of regime change or the United States in favor of democracy. It was a regime change but not in favor of democracy because the shah was the cruel tyrant who ruled over Iran for a long time. Stephen Kinzer has written a book, *All the Shah's Men*. He was a journalist in the Middle East. His book is a dramatic and interesting account of what happened in that coup.

Let me read you something. "The people of England have been led in Mesopotamia into a trap from which it will be hard to escape with dignity and honour. They have been tricked into it by a steady withholding of information. The Baghdad communiqués are belated, insincere, incomplete. Things have been far worse than we have been told, our administration more bloody and inefficient than the public knows. It is a disgrace to our imperial record, and may soon be too inflamed for any ordinary cure. We are to-day not far from a disaster. . . . our unfortunate troops, Indian and British, under hard conditions of climate and supply are policing an immense area, paying dearly every day in lives for the willfully wrong policy of the civil administration in Baghdad but the responsibility, in this case, is not on the army which has acted only upon the request of the civil authorities." That was written by T. E. Lawrence, the fabled Lawrence of Arabia, in the Sunday Times of London, August 22, 1920. So if you just changed a couple of those words around today, it could sound like a dispatch coming from Robert Fisk or John Pilger.

They should show *Lawrence of Arabia*, again and again, because although its main intention was not to make a political and historical point, the point is vividly made in that film. And Peter O'Toole, playing Lawrence, expresses the sentiment, actually doesn't express it as strongly and as clearly as in that quotation that you read from him. But certainly the film makes quite clear that he was dismayed by the betrayal of the Arabs, with the British, of course, claiming, as the Americans are now claiming in Iraq, that they will enter into the Middle East and that they will do the mayhem that they're doing for the benefit of the Arab people. T. E. Lawrence understood that.

Eqbal Ahmad says of that imperial settlement at the end of World War I, when the Ottoman Empire was picked apart by the British and by the French, that "tribes were given flags" and were kind of turned into imperial petrol pumps.

That process goes on. It's a classic imperial story of people being used against their own interests and against their own people. Because an imperial power can never succeed in conquering a people only with its resources. It always needs internal allies. It always needs people in the conquered country that it can bribe or coerce into being what came to be known in World War II as quislings, people who would betray their own people. Vidkun Quisling, a Norwegian, was the Nazi puppet ruler of Norway. We see this operating in every imperial situation. The British used Indians against

Indians in maintaining control of India. The United States in Vietnam used the South Vietnamese army in trying to defeat the revolutionary movement in Vietnam.

But generally, historically, and this would be instructive for people looking at the situation today in Iraq, a point is reached when those domestic allies of the imperial power are no longer reliable, when they will not do the job. They do not come to it with the same enthusiasm that the imperial power comes to it, and so you find that they defect, they desert. And this is, in fact, what is happening now with the Iraqi soldiers that the United States has enlisted to help control Iraq.

Peter Balakian has written a book called The Burning Tigris. *It's about the Armenian genocide, and the U.S. response to it in particular. He says, "Memory is a moral act." To remember, to recall history is an act of affirmation.*

That's an interesting way of putting it, that remembering, yes, is a moral act because without remembering, you are subject to somebody else's remembering or somebody else's forgetting. Without remembering, you are subject to the immorality of the people who control information and who control history. And so memory, then, when you insist on your own memory rather than the memory of the people in power, then it becomes a moral act.

Milan Kundera, the Czech writer, wrote The Book of Laughter and Forgetting. *It opens with Communist Party leaders "on the balcony of a Baroque palace in Prague. . . . The Party propaganda section put out hundreds of thousands of copies" of that photo. A few years later, one of those leaders had fallen from grace and was removed from power. And he was airbrushed out of that particular photograph. An interesting concept, airbrushing history. And then Kundera says, "the struggle of man against power is the struggle of memory against forgetting."*

Absolutely true. Laughter is the enemy of tyranny. I remember that in Kundera's "The Joke," he has somebody in Czechoslovakia just send a postcard to somebody else with a joke on it, and that is enough to land that person in jail. You don't joke in a totalitarian state. Kundera, I think, does a service by reminding us of the importance of memory. And yes, those in power want us to forget because without memory we were born yesterday and thus have no way of checking up on what is told to us by the government and the corporate media. Memory—history—is a reminder of past lies, deceits, and also a reminder that seemingly powerless people can defeat those who rule them, if they persist.

You might not even be able to joke in the United States. Did you hear what happened in Boulder, Colorado, with a high school rock band?

Tell me.

A group originally called The Taliband later became The Coalition of the Willing. They were performing Bob Dylan's "Masters of War" in rehearsals. And apparently someone took offense to it and called in to a Denver radio talk show, saying that the kids in Boulder are threatening George Bush's life. The next day the Secret Service visited the band members and interrogated them.

That is one of those bizarre incidents that are happening more and more in the United States. Now that you remind me of it, I did read about that. "Masters of War" is a very powerful statement. Let's not pretend that it is a gentle and innocent statement about war because Dylan says, in effect, to the masters of war, When you die, I will celebrate. And that, in association with Bush being president, of course, is enough to suggest to the FBI and the Justice Department, "Oh, we mustn't talk about our leaders in that way. We mustn't talk about masters of war in that raw, bold way that Dylan talked about it."

History is contentious. There have been fierce arguments about the Enola Gay exhibit and the atomic bombing of Japan. But particularly Vietnam has been a lightning rod for not just debate but extreme rancor, vitriol, and recrimination. What is it about the Vietnam War that so riles people's sensitivities?

Vietnam was an especially dramatic and searing event in American history, one reason being that it was the first time that a war fought by the United States was met by a national movement of protest, which grew so powerful and had such an effect on the administration that it was forced to reckon with it. And that anti-war movement played an important part in bringing the war to an end, so much so that after the war ended, after the United States withdrew its troops from Vietnam, the administration of the United States was determined to, as they put it, get rid of the Vietnam syndrome.

Syndrome is a term that very often is associated with sickness. And what was sick about the Vietnam situation, in the eyes of the establishment, was that it brought forth a huge movement against war and militarism and against the establishment, a huge disaffection from the government. All the polls taken right after the end of the war showed that the public had lost faith in Congress, in the president, in the FBI, in the CIA, in the military. This was threatening and horrifying to the administration. They determined from that point on to do something about this Vietnam syndrome. And since then, they have been trying very hard to destroy the memory of Vietnam because the memory of Vietnam is a memory of the United States killing several million people in Vietnam for reasons that, after a while, people understood were false. And the memory of that, and the memory of the movement against the war, the memory of soldiers refusing to fight, the memory of B52 pilots refusing to fly anymore—they don't want that memory to exist; they don't want that memory to have an effect.

So Vietnam is an instance of American history that they are trying to either remove from the American consciousness or to give it a different kind of history, where we forget about what we really did to Vietnam and we think of it as a heroic thing. And I must say that John Kerry himself played into that, unfortunately, in the presidential campaign because instead of emphasizing his true heroism in the war, that is, after the war, when he spoke out against the war, he put that aside and ignored that and instead talked about his military heroism in the war, thus doing what the establishment wanted, and that is, to keep the memory of the Vietnam War as a memory of military heroism rather than a memory of national disgrace.

Kerry said that he was proud to have defended the United States in Vietnam. I don't remember Vietnam attacking the United States that it needed that kind of defense.

What you said just reminded me of something that happened when I was speaking to that prep school in Tampa. You were saying that John Kerry said he was defending the United States, and you pointed out that you weren't aware that Vietnam had attacked the United

States. And one of the questions put to me by a student at Tampa Prep was explaining our going into Iraq, saying, "Well, they attacked us, so we had to attack them." And, of course, I just had to explain gently that, no, they did not attack us.

But the word *defense* is one of those words that is used again and again in an Orwellian way, and that is, you go into a country and you call it defense. You send troops halfway around the world to invade another country, and you call it defense. It's interesting that at the end of World War II we changed the name of the Department of War to the Department of Defense. In fact, just at that point when we were going to inaugurate a series of aggressive wars, from 1945 on, that is, in Korea, Vietnam, Panama, Grenada, and Iraq and so on, just at the point when we truly became a war-making nation in a large sense, we changed the name from *war* to *defense*.

During the 2004 presidential campaign, Kerry's military record, and particularly his testimony on war crimes before J. William Fulbright's Senate Foreign Relations Committee, became the focus of much attention. The infamous Swift boat ads were generously funded and appeared not only many, many times as commercials but also as news items. So they got double play: You not only saw the commercials, but then the media would report on them and show them again. Let me show you something that I picked up on the campaign trail. It's a Vietnamese currency note with a picture of John Kerry, calling him "The great war hero of the Viet Cong."

This is a very common propaganda tool, to take anybody who criticizes a war that the United States is engaged in and to say therefore that that person is in league with the enemy. Of course, that then not only becomes a basis for maligning the person, as was done in the case of John Kerry in the election campaign, but, more seriously, it becomes the case for putting people in jail, for claiming that people are serving the purpose of the enemy simply by criticizing the United States. That's what happened in World War I, where people like Eugene Debs, but many other people, a thousand other people who criticized American entrance into the war, were then indicted under the Espionage Act. Interestingly, when the public heard that they were indicted under the Espionage Act, they assumed they were guilty of espionage, which means you are serving the interests of another country. But what they were simply doing was criticizing American entrance into the war. That was seen as tantamount to espionage, to treason, and therefore deserving of being imprisoned. We are right now in the United States creating that kind of atmosphere, where anybody who is critical of American war is going to be in danger.

People like the actor Danny Glover, the writer Terry Tempest Williams, have lost speaking engagements because of their position on Iraq.

I pay tribute to people like Danny Glover, who has not been intimidated, or Terry Tempest Williams or so many of the other people in the arts who have spoken out against the war. I remember Jessica Lange, who was speaking in Spain at a film festival shortly after the war began in Afghanistan. Somebody asked this Academy Award–winning actress what she thought of the Bush administration. And she said, "I despise the Bush administration and everything it stands for." It caused a flurry, of course, but she continues to work and speak out. And I notice now that her husband, Sam Shepard, has a play on Broadway, *The God of Hell*, which is his first overtly political play of the fifty plays that he's written. And in one of his interviews he attributes the political nature of his play to the influence of his wife, Jessica Lange.

When you look at the American political landscape, the paradoxes and contradictions are also particularly acute. And I'm thinking of something you said in one of your talks. You said Nixon broke into an office building and he was impeached. Three decades later, Bush breaks into a country and nothing happens. Yet, at the same time, there is a peace movement, there are demonstrations. What's happened between those two events?

It's interesting, this use of language for criminals breaking and entering. Yes, breaking and entering into a house, you go to jail. Breaking and entering into a country, you get elected. And what's happening now is that Bush, winning 51 percent of the vote, has taken 100 percent of control of the country, of all of its branches, of every aspect of government. This is a very dangerous situation for American democracy.

As you think back to that period of the 1960s and 1970s, maybe one could say that the caliber of the leaders in the Senate was significantly different, better, higher, than what we have today. At that time there was J. William Fulbright, Frank Church, Wayne Morse, Ernest Gruening, and a few others who asked pointed questions.

It's true that we today in the Senate and in the House do not have the voices that we had at that time. I think it's fair to say that the voices at that time were not as courageous as they might have been. Fulbright was bold enough to hold hearings on the war and to give a platform to people who spoke out against the war. And Gruening and Morse voted against the Tonkin Gulf Resolution. Congress responded late. It took a strong anti-war movement in the country to finally move Congress, just toward the end of the war, to pass the War Powers Act, which albeit in not a very strong way attempted to limit the powers of the president and began to cut off funds for the war, which was coming to an end at that point. Today we have very few powerful voices in Congress or the Senate.

I was happy to see that Cynthia McKinney, the African American woman in Georgia, regained her seat in the House after being pushed out by a coalition of powerful moneyed interests, because she is one of the people who has been absolutely unyielding in her criticism of American foreign policy. I remember that in the first Gulf War in 1991, Cynthia McKinney was one of the few people in Congress who spoke out against the war in Iraq at that time. So there are a few people like her. But we still lack in Congress real opposition. The Democratic Party itself has been pitifully weak. It has not been a true opposition party. And I think this suggests the need in the United States for a political movement that will do what the Democratic Party seems incapable of doing, and that is, to create a real political opposition to the policies of the administration.

Your 1967 book Vietnam: The Logic of Withdrawal *was reissued by South End Press. I was reading some of the exchanges in the Senate Foreign Relations Committee that you reproduce there. And although there are no such hearings going on now, it almost replicates a lot of the media commentary about how we cannot just quit and run from Iraq, that our prestige would suffer, we would lose credibility. What do these things mean? What is prestige? What is credibility?*

That's an interesting point because those statements are made again and again, from war to war to war, that we must continue doing this because if we don't continue doing this, we will lose standing, lose prestige, that other countries in the world will lose respect for us. I think what they really mean is that other countries will stop fearing us. The truth is that the United States in general does not get the respect of other countries in the world, but it instills fear in other countries, fear that they will lose economic benefits given to them by the United States. As a result, some of them go along. But, of course, those words *prestige* and *fear* need to be examined to see what they mean because if you looked at them in moral terms, you would ask, What prestige adheres to a government that conducts an immoral war? What respect does the United States get from the rest of the world when it engages in such a war?

What's interesting in this case, and I think this is really unprecedented in the case of Iraq, is that on the eve of the war the world as a whole rose up everywhere and protested against the U.S. entrance into the war, making it clear that by going into the war the United States was losing the respect, losing whatever prestige it had in the world. So these can become words just thrown out. Unfortunately, people in the media, journalists, use these words again and again to excuse what the United States is doing. And those words become substitutes for discussing the realities of the war. Instead of explaining why morally the United States needs to wage war, they are saying it needs to wage war to maintain its prestige, suggesting that even if the war is wrong, the important thing is to continue doing it so that people won't look on the United States as a country that cut and run, as they put it.

Talk more about this mystical word prestige. *France occupied Algeria for more than one hundred thirty years. For the last eight years of that occupation, it waged a brutal and vicious counterinsurgency war resulting in the death of perhaps a million Algerians. France under de Gaulle in 1962 left Algeria. Did France's prestige collapse?*

I think you do something very important there, and that is you use history to demolish this notion that if an imperial power releases its hold on a colonized country, therefore it loses prestige. And, of course, the answer to your question is no. No, France did not lose prestige. Did the Soviet Union lose prestige when it left Afghanistan? I don't think so. And as far as the United States in Vietnam, the United States did not lose prestige because it left Vietnam. It lost prestige when it was bombing Vietnam.

There is a brilliant film made by Gillo Pontecorvo called The Battle of Algiers. *It's a classic example of cinema vérité, with hand-held cameras. In some sequences you think you're actually watching a documentary about the Algerian resistance to the French. It seems that there are some similarities between what the French were doing in Algeria and what the Americans are doing in Iraq: The Americans will win all the battles, they have overwhelming force, they use torture, as the French did, and is depicted in that film. But ultimately the resistance is able to drive them out.*

The film has gotten more attention recently because a lot of people have recognized the similarities between the French war against the Algerians and what is happening today in Iraq. As you pointed out, and I've seen this point made in the discussion of torture in Iraq, the French justified their torture the way the American military justifies their torture, and the way, you might say, that some people have justified Israeli torture. I think of Alan Dershowitz, who came out and defended the use of torture under certain circumstances.

What's happened in Iraq, and what happened in Algeria, should be a lesson to the American establishment that they cannot win this war in Iraq. They may win battles, and they will kill a lot of people, as they are doing, but ultimately the United States is going to have to get out of Iraq, just as ultimately the French had to get out of Algeria. But they are not going to recognize it by themselves. They are not going to recognize it unless they reach a point when the resistance clearly is not going to stop, and also, when the American people demand that the United States stop the war. That's what it will take.

If you were to write The Logic of Withdrawal *today in terms of Iraq, what would you write?*

As I did then, in 1967. I must say, mine was the first book on the Vietnam War that called for American withdrawal. There had been a number of books critical of American intervention in Vietnam, but none of them called for withdrawal. Withdrawal was considered a radical step. And if I were talking about the situation in Iraq today, I would deal with the same kinds of arguments that were raised at that time, because at that time also it was said, just as you indicated before, that American prestige was involved, credibility, and also— and this is an important point that has to be made—if we leave Vietnam, they said, there will be a bloodbath, terrible things will happen.

To me, that's the argument that you see again and again. Whenever something atrocious is done, it is excused on the grounds that it is preventing an even more atrocious act. The bombing of Hiroshima, one of the great atrocities of history, was justified by the fact that if they did not bomb Hiroshima and Nagasaki, a greater calamity would occur, and that is, a million people would die—and these figures were ridiculously thrown out into the air—because then we would have to invade Japan. So the American people then, and, unfortunately, most Americans today, still accept the justification for the bombing of Hiroshima on the grounds that it prevented an even greater number of deaths.

A lot of truth is lost in this. But one of the things that is lost in this is a simple concept. And that is, when you commit an atrocity in the immediate in order to prevent something in the future, the atrocity you commit is certain, the future is uncertain. Nobody knew what would happen in Vietnam after we left. Nobody knew what would happen if we didn't drop the bomb on Hiroshima. And nobody really knows what will happen in Iraq. What we do know is what is happening in Iraq right now is a catastrophe. We cannot justify continuing the catastrophe by saying something more catastrophic will happen.

You see the yellow ribbons with the words "Support Our Troops." What do you think of that?

Everyone cares about young people sent to war. "Support Our Troops" therefore does not have any meaning until you give it some. To some people it means "support the war." That's what it means to Bush and company. But supporting the war means keeping those troops in danger of losing their lives or arms or legs or eyesight. The best way to support the troops is to save their lives, to get them out of the war. Therefore the U.S. government is certainly not supporting the troops. Exactly the opposite. It is dooming them to death or disfigurement or mental anguish. The only real way to support the troops is to bring them home. And then take care of them, physically, mentally, morally. Which is what governments don't do when the soldiers come home. Note how the latest Bush budget short-changes funds for veterans. And note how they refuse to accept (as with Agent Orange in Vietnam or depleted uranium in the first Gulf War) that our military activities have had terrible consequences for our soldiers and their families.

"Stay the course" is another empty slogan that is mindlessly repeated. Iraq is a disaster. It reminds me of the definition of fanaticism: When you discover you are going in the wrong direction, you double your speed.

In your essay "The Problem Is Civil Obedience," reprinted in Voices of A People's History of the United States, *you write, "our topic is topsy-turvy: civil disobedience. As soon as you say the topic is civil disobedience, you are saying our problem is civil disobedience. That is not our problem. . . . Our problem is civil obedience. Our problem is the numbers of people all over the world who have obeyed the dictates of the leaders of their governments and have gone to war, and millions have been killed because of this obedience."*

This was, of course, in the midst of the Vietnam War when I was engaged in this debate, interestingly enough, at Johns Hopkins, where I am going next week to speak again. And maybe I will remind them again at Johns Hopkins of the need for civil disobedience and of the dangers of obedience. But it struck me at that time, speaking during the Vietnam War, how people who committed civil disobedience in protesting the war were going to jail. And people who committed civil obedience, and that is by obeying the dictates of the government and going to war and killing people, of course that was the patriotic thing to do. But I remember some wise person talking about Adam and Eve in biting the apple, saying the human race came into being by an act of disobedience, and the human race will go out of existence by an act of obedience.

In New York I picked up a postcard with a bust of Comrade Lenin. It says, "No Empire Lasts Forever." Actually it's a promo for a cable company that says, "Especially One That Keeps You Waiting 5 Hours for a Repairman." So no empire lasts forever. I was thinking about that in relation to one of your columns in The Progressive, *called "Humpty Dumpty Will Fall." It's about empires in the past that were full of hubris, self-importance, and a sense of infallibility. To illustrate your point, as you sometimes do, you bring in something from the world of art, in this case Aeschylus's play* The Persians.

I was inspired to do that because at that time in New York they were putting on *The Persians* by Aeschylus. Written in the late fifth century B.C., it may be the earliest surviving play in Western literature. It's an elegy to a passing empire, Persia, and a warning to a new one, Greece. Of course, the Greeks have so much to say about war, having engaged in it so much themselves. And the Greek playwrights played the kind of role during the Greek wars that we, I think, hope our own artists and our own playwrights would play today. Euripides, Sophocles, Aeschylus, and Aristophanes were bitter opponents of war. In *The Persians*, we see the fall of another seemingly invincible empire. The chorus recognizes the new reality:

> All those years we spent jubilant,
> seeing the trifling, cowering
> world from the height of our
> shining saddles, brawling our might
> across the earth as we forged an

> *empire, I never questioned.*
> *Surely we were doing the right thing. . . .*
> *It seemed so clear—our fate was to rule.*
> *That's what I thought at the time.*
> *But perhaps we were merely*
> *deafened for years by the din*
> *of our own empire-building,*
> *the shouts of battle,*
> *the clanging of swords,*
> *the cries of victory.*

I thought it was so true that we here in the United States can be deafened by all the stories every day in the newspapers, the battles that we're fighting, and the heroism of our marines fighting their way into the streets of Falluja, and forgetting, then, what war is really like. I concluded that essay with the following:

> *Those of us who become momentarily disheartened by "the cries*
> *of victory" should remind ourselves of that long history in which*
> *seemingly insurmountable power fell not only of its own unbear-*
> *able weight, but also because of the resistance of those who re-*
> *fused finally to bear that weight, and would not give up.*

Your new book is Voices of A People's History of the United States. *In what way is it different from* A People's History of the United States?

Voices of A People's History *originated with sort of a collective idea that came to me, Anthony Arnove, and Daniel Simon of Seven Stories Press. And that is that my book, A People's History, which has been read by an awful lot of people, has in it a lot of quotes and snatches of commentary by various people from fugitive slaves and angry women to antiwar protesters and striking workers. Our idea was that what people found most interesting in A *People's History* were other people's words and not my own words. So we decided to take these little bits, these snatches that were in my book, of which there were many, and expand on them. *Voices* has a minimum of words from me and from Anthony, just introducing the presentation of the words of Las Casas, Thoreau, Debs, Helen Keller, going right up to the present day with the Rodriguez family saying they'd lost their son in the explosions in the Twin Towers. And they did not want the government to retaliate for their son's death by killing other people.

One of the other voices you feature is Paul Robeson. A postage stamp was recently issued in his honor. On the back of the stamp you get a little biography. It says of him: "A world-renowned actor, singer, activist, and, athlete. Paul Robeson (1898–1976) was a man ahead of his time. Whether performing spirituals and folk songs or interpreting Shakespeare's Othello, Robeson infused his life and work with his principled stand against racism and his outspoken commitment to social justice." All of which is true, but maybe space didn't allow for a little more elaboration on some of the things that happened to this remarkable artist.

I was surprised that the post office department went as far as it did in issuing a stamp in his honor because, after all, Robeson was condemned by the U.S. government, Robeson was denied a passport, Robeson was threatened with prison, Robeson basically was blacklisted in the United States. This famous actor and singer was called before the House Committee on Un-American Activities and questioned about his political beliefs. He was treated shamefully.

Earlier, you talked about the expunging of certain things from history, about people and events left out of history. Here's an example of that. Paul Robeson was an all-American football player. The annual book that carried the pictures of all the all-American football teams, the year that he was on the all-American team carried a photo of the members of the all-American team, but Robeson's picture had been removed from that picture. I tell you that only to show how bizarre and how absolutely ridiculous are the lengths to which a kind of hysterical society will go.

In Voices *you include his unread statement before the House Committee on Un-American Activities on June 12, 1956.*

You said unread statement because the House Committee on Un-American Activities would not allow him to read the statement he wanted to read. They wanted to question him, they wanted to interrogate him, they wanted to ask him about his political beliefs or his connections with Communists and so on, but they would not allow him to make a statement. Such a perfect illustration. A committee that calls itself a Committee on Un-American Activities yet engages in the most un-American activity of all—suppressing somebody's freedom of speech.

You include two songs from Woody Guthrie, "Ludlow Massacre" and "This Land Is Your Land," the latter being widely known. "Ludlow Massacre" had a big impact on you when you first heard it.

It startled me because I had never learned anything about the Ludlow massacre. I had never learned anything about the Colorado coal strike of 1913, 1914, which culminated in the Ludlow massacre, that is, the massacre of miners and killing of women and children, the burning of a tent colony by the National Guard in Colorado. Nothing like that had ever been mentioned in any of my courses or in any of my books. But that led me to investigate further and to do research on the Ludlow massacre and led me to write about it, as I have done.

Did you hear it on the radio?

I heard it on an old 78-rpm record sometime in the early 1950s. I'm sort of dubious that it would have been played on the radio. I'm not sure if it ever was.

In recent months, I visited Trinidad, Colorado, the site of the Ludlow Massacre, and there are some things to report. One is that the actual monument built by the United Mine Workers where you see the names of the slain, including those of babies, has been vandalized. That monument is just off I-25. Then I went to the nearby highway rest stop. There is a permanent photographic exhibit. And I'm reading the Colorado Historical Society text of what happened at Ludlow. It says, On April 20, 1914, "shots rang out" and "fire swept the camp." There was no mention that Rockefeller, who owned the mine, paid to put down the strike by force. So, there again is the use of the passive voice, "shots rang out," and "fire swept the camp," people were killed. (Postscript: The Ludlow monument was repaired and rededicated in June 2005.)

That's so often a way of covering up the responsibility for these tragedies, acting as if they came out of nowhere and removing these events from the context of class struggle and the context of state power and the link between state power and corporate power. Because that's exactly what we saw in Colorado: the link between the Colorado Fuel and Iron Corporation, Rockefeller's company, and the government of the state of Colorado, which called out the National Guard at the behest of Rockefeller. He then paid the National Guard because the state government couldn't afford to. So we had this collaboration between the state and the corporate entity. This kind of revelation about how American society works, about how the state works in collaboration with corporate power, is something they do not want to publicize.

The other Woody Guthrie song is "This Land Is Your Land." It was written in 1940 and was supposedly a socialist response to "God Bless America." I understand that parts of Woody Guthrie's songs are often suppressed. I heard Steve Earle in Sante Fe, New Mexico, sing those missing stanzas in which Guthrie sings about signs saying "Private Property" and poor people standing on line at the Relief Office.

> As they stood hungry, I stood there wondering if
> This land was made for you and me.

Another musician featured in Voices, *someone in the tradition of Guthrie and Dylan, is Bruce Springsteen and his 1995 album* The Ghost of Tom Joad. *Tom Joad being the protagonist in Steinbeck's* The Grapes of Wrath.

The Ghost of Tom Joad. I think it is important that Bruce Springsteen should write songs about that because we need to recall *The Grapes of Wrath*. We need to recall what was important about *The Grapes of Wrath*. We need to recall that there are millions and millions of people in this country who live in poverty, are homeless, who live in ghettos, who live in places that are really unfit for human habitation, or people who have to migrate from one part of the country to another in search of work. These facts about American society are hidden, especially in time of war, when the headlines are all about what is happening in the war, and at the same time, nobody is understanding that Americans are suffering and that the money that goes for the war might be used to alleviate some of that suffering. So I think the kind of class consciousness that is represented in Springsteen's songs, and of course in Steinbeck's novel, needs to be revived in the United States today.

8

A WORLD WITHOUT BORDERS

Cambridge, Massachusetts
February 7, 2005

Politicians use history as a kind of mystical element or device. We often hear that the United States is called upon by history to do certain things in the world.

History is always a good entity to call upon if you are hesitant to call upon God because they both play the same role. They are both abstractions; they are both actually meaningless until you invest them with meaning. I've noticed that President Bush calls upon God a lot. I think he's hesitant to call upon history because I think the word *history* throws him; he's not quite sure what to do with it, but he's more familiar with God.

History is invoked because nobody can say what history really has ordained for you, just as nobody can say what God has ordained for you. It's an empty vessel, which you can fill in whatever way you can. So you can say that history has decided that the United States will be the great leader of the world and that American values, values being another empty vessel that you can fill with anything you want, will be transmitted to the rest of the world. So you can fill history, that abstraction history, with anything you want, use it whenever you want.

Political leaders, I guess, suppose that the population is as mystified by the word *history* as they are by the word *God*, and that therefore they will accept whatever interpretation of history is given to them. So the political leaders feel free to declare that history is on their side, and the way is open for them to use it in whatever manner they want.

Donald Macedo, in the introduction to your book On Democratic Education, *mentions the Tom Paxton song "What Did You Learn in School Today?" He quotes a couple of the lyrics. "I learned that Washington never told a lie / I learned that soldiers seldom die / I learned that everybody's free." What does a democratic education mean to you?*

To me, a democratic education means many things: It means what you learn in the classroom; it means what you learn outside the classroom; it means not only the content of what you learn, but it means the atmosphere in which you learn it; it refers to the relationship between teacher and student. All of these elements of education can be democratic or undemocratic.

And so for the content of education to be democratic, it must take its cue from the idea of democracy, the idea that people will determine their own destiny. And therefore, it means students have a part in this. Students as human beings, as citizens in a democracy, have the right to determine their lives, have a right to play a role in the society. And therefore, a democratic education gives students the kind of information that will enable them to have a power of their own in the society.

And what that means is really to give the students a kind of education that, going into history, suggests to the students that historically there have been many, many ways in which ordinary people—people as ordinary as the student feels as he or she is sitting in the classroom—can play a part in the making of history, in the development of their society. So that a democratic education in that sense is an education that gives the student examples in history of where ordinary people have shown their power and their energy in not only reshaping their own lives but playing a part in how society works. That would be the substance of a democratic education, or part of the substance of a democratic education.

And then the relationship of the student to the teacher. There is democracy in the classroom. The understanding given to the student that the student has a right to challenge the teacher, that the student has a right to express ideas of his or her own. That education is an interchange between the experiences of the teacher, which may be far greater than the student in certain ways, and the experiences of the student, which are unique, since every student has a unique life experience, one which a teacher has not had, and therefore the student is in a position to throw into the educational reservoir of the class the student's own experience. So the interchange between student and teacher, the free inquiry that is promulgated in the classroom, a spirit of equality in the classroom, to me that is part of a democratic education.

By the time you started teaching at Boston University, you were fairly well known as someone who was active in the civil rights and anti-Vietnam War movements. What about structural relationship between the pedagogue, in your case, someone who has a reputation, and students, who may think: Ooh, this is Howard Zinn. He's so famous.

That is a situation that exists, which the teacher cannot totally control. The student comes into the classroom and here is the teacher.

Even if the teacher has not written books, even if the teacher is not well known, this is the teacher. The teacher is up there, the teacher has the podium and the platform, and the teacher has degrees. And so there is this immediate situation, which creates a possibility of subservience to the teacher. Therefore, the more the teacher has the reputation of not only being a teacher but perhaps of writing books and being well known, the more this is so, I think the greater is the obligation on the teacher to try to break down the barrier that is created by what may be the student's awe of this know-it-all who stands up there in front of the classroom.

So for me, in my case, it was very important to make it clear to the students that I didn't know everything, to make it clear that I learned what I'm giving them just as they will learn, that I was not born with the knowledge that I'm imparting to them, that knowledge isn't given by God or by history, knowledge is acquired in very ordinary ways, ways in which the student can acquire also. So it becomes important to let the student know that and to let the student know that the teacher is fallible.

And it was also important in my case, because my views on the world were always partisan views, that is, views that express certain definite values, for me to make it clear to the student that my views were not to be taken as the gospel, that they were my views. That knowledge is subjective, that history is subjective, that there are many different interpretations, and that mine was one of them, and that all that I was asking of the student is that the student consider my views as part of the marketplace of ideas, in which there were many views. And all that I was doing was starting from a premise that the marketplace of ideas is not a free marketplace, that the marketplace of ideas, like the economic marketplace, is dominated by certain powerful entities, and therefore, that all that I was doing was wheeling my little pushcart into the marketplace and saying to the student, "Here, sample this, and see if this makes sense."

There are contrasting perspectives on what the term well educated *means. What does it mean to you?*

There is an orthodox view of what it means to be well educated, and the orthodox view is that a person is well educated who has gone through all the realms of education. And the higher up you go, the more degrees you have, the better educated you are. The more knowledge you have, the more facts you have acquired, the more languages you can speak, the more important people you can quote, the more reading you have done, all of that falls within the orthodox definition of higher education, of education itself, being well educated. And, of course, a lot of that is legitimate; that is, to me a lot of that makes sense.

But it is not sufficient for me. That is, to me being well educated means not just sort of a mastery of information, not just a quantity of information, but to me being well educated means being educated in what is important and what is not important, educated in having a sense of proportion about what knowledge is significant, what knowledge is not significant, what knowledge is trivial and what knowledge has very powerful ramifications, what knowledge can contribute to the betterment of society and what knowledge is really just sort of static information lying there, whether in the book or in the head, but which has no energy that it propels into society to have an effect on whatever is going on in society.

How do you as a teacher foster that sense of questioning and skepticism, and how do you avoid its going over to its first cousin, cynicism?

Skepticism, being one of the most important qualities that you can educate a student in, I think arises from having the student realize that what has been seen as holy is not holy, what has been revered is not necessarily to be revered. That the acts of the nation that have been romanticized and idealized and presented as marvelous acts, those in fact deserve to be scrutinized and looked at critically. That the actions of the country in which you live, the ideas of the people who have been held up to you as important thinkers, to show the flaws in those ideas, to show the flaws in those actions.

And once a student has learned to be skeptical in one area, then that skepticism carries over. I remember that a friend of mine, Bill Bigelow, who teaches history on the West Coast and who was teaching his kids in middle school to be skeptical of what they had learned about Columbus as the great hero and liberator, expander of civilization, that one of his students—her name was Rebecca—said to him, "Well, if I have been so misled about Columbus, I wonder now, what else have I been misled about?" So that is education in skepticism.

Sure, that can carry over into cynicism, but I think the way to avoid that is to give a student information that shows that those ideas, those people, those actions that a student has learned to be skeptical of have also been the objects of other people's skepticism and also have been the object of other people's reaction, that these ideas and these actions have not gone unchallenged. The student should learn the history of such challenges to show that the student who is thinking about this is not the first person to be skeptical of this, and that people have not just reacted to their own skepticism with passivity and with cynicism, but to show that very often in history people have shown their critical understanding of society by rebelling against what they saw and by organizing to change what they saw was wrong.

*When you taught at Spelman College, and later at Boston University,
you were teaching kids just coming out of high school. And they come
with a lot of baggage, a lot of embedded ideas. How difficult was it for
you to reach them?*

In the case of teaching at Spelman College, there was a special factor, and that was simply that my students were African American,
my students were black, and I was a white teacher. I was one of a few
white teachers in this all-black college. I was for most of the students
in my class the first white teacher they had ever encountered.

And therefore, aside from the usual problem of growing to de-
velop a relationship of trust with students, between students and
teachers, there was a special problem in this case of black students
growing up in a segregated society in which the idea of white su-
premacy, although they didn't believe it, was widespread—of persuading such students that they could trust me.

That's something that could not be done overnight. That's something that could be done only—and this was what I tried to do—by
having them realize that my values and ideas were very different
from those of the white-supremacist society they had grown up in,
that I believed in the equality of human beings, and that I took the
claims of democracy seriously. And to try to break down the barrier
between us not only by what I said in the classroom but by how I
behaved toward them in the classroom by my accepting of who they
were by not indicating that their education had been poor, which it
very often was, by not making them feel that they were coming into
this classroom handicapped. So I had to break down the barrier
between us not only by what I said but by my attitude toward them
as students in the classroom.

And also—and this became important teaching at Spelman

College—by showing them that outside the classroom I was not retreating into my home and my study, that outside the classroom I was involved in the world outside. I was involved in the social struggle that related to their lives. And that when they decided to participate in this struggle, when my students decided to move out of the classroom and to go into the city of Atlanta and try to desegregate the public library or when they decided to follow the example of the four students in Greensboro, North Carolina, in early 1960 and decided to sit in at places in Atlanta to break down the barrier of segregation, that I was with them, I was supporting them, I was helping them, I was walking on picket lines with them, I was engaging in demonstrations with them, I was sitting in with them. And that more than anything, I think, created an atmosphere of trust, of democracy in our relationship.

When you were growing up and attending public schools in New York, were there any influential, memorable teachers?

Most of my memorable teachers gave me bad memories. I think the first time I was struck by a teacher in a way that made me admire this teacher was in high school, when I had an English teacher who was not only very interesting in the classroom and not only gave us things to read that were exciting, whether it was poetry or fiction, but was a person of conscience. I learned—and consider, this was the 1930s at the time of the depression, a time of rising radicalism in the United States—that this teacher was out in the world demonstrating, participating in some mysterious cause that I didn't understand.

But this said something to me about this teacher as a human being and also suggested to me something that I kept with me for many years later, when I became a teacher: that it's very important to a student to learn that a teacher has a life outside the classroom and to learn about the teacher as a human being outside the classroom, and that this has an educational value, which is very special and very different from whatever value is in the knowledge imparted in the classroom.

Some Americans have conflicted views about intellectuals. Richard Hofstadter wrote a book called Anti-Intellectualism in American Life. *Often intellectuals are the butt of late-night-TV-talk-show jokes: they're out of touch. What ideological purpose do those kinds of views serve?*

You must remember, caricatures are always based on some reality; if there wasn't some reality to these caricatures, they wouldn't have any effect. The caricaturing of intellectuals as being ineffectual, not connected with reality, is a convenient way of putting anybody who studies, teaches, brings ideas forward, writes, sort of outside the margins of acceptability and is a way of taking something that is true of some intellectuals and applying it to all intellectuals. It serves the same purpose that stereotypes of all kinds serve, whether they're racial or religious or national stereotypes. So the stereotype of an intellectual therefore gets in the way of people who devote their lives to writing and teaching, gets in the way of their gaining acceptance, especially among people who themselves are not intellectuals and therefore are easily persuaded that intellectuals are not to be trusted.

You've been a lifelong reader from the time you found Tarzan and the Jewels of Opar *in the street with the first few pages torn out. Later, your parents got you the complete collection of Charles Dickens's nov-*

els. *Today we live in an age of sound bites and eye bites, quick bursts of information. What's the value of reading?*

It's interesting that even in this age of sound bites, as you say, even in this age when television has taken over the lives of so many people, especially the younger people in this generation, where therefore there is less time to read, and less opportunity to read, still, even in this time, books are important and people turn to books. And, obviously, people are still reading. Millions of books are sold.

And I do believe that books have a lasting impact that television and movies, the sound bites of radio, do not have. Of course, I realize I'm talking to a person in alternative radio. But I do believe that there is an effect in reading that is more profound than the effect of watching or listening, even though those may be very influential. And, of course, I've spoken to people who are very much affected by something they saw on television, some movie they saw, some lecture they listened to on radio, some person who said something on radio and awakened something in them. And yet, whenever I've spoken to people about books that they've read, it seemed to me that the effect of the books was much more long-lasting and profound.

I'll put it another way—and I don't know if my experience agrees with the experience of other people—I have talked to people, young people especially, who would say to me, "This book changed my life." I remember sitting in a cafeteria in Hawaii across from a student at the University of Hawaii, and the student had before her a copy of *The Color Purple* by Alice Walker. And since Alice Walker had been my student at Spelman College—of course, I didn't immediately say, "That's my student"—I sort of cautiously said, "Oh, you're reading *The Color Purple*. What do you think of it?" And the student said, "This book changed my life." And that startled me, a book that changed your life.

And also, I must say, in all modesty, that I have run into a number of students who have read *A People's History of the United States*, and who said, in ways that I first did not believe but I'm almost beginning to believe it now, "You know, your book changed my life."

There are books, I think, that changed my life. You mentioned Dickens. And, yes, I think reading Dickens changed my life. Reading Steinbeck's *The Grapes of Wrath* changed my life. Reading Upton Sinclair, yes, changed my life.

Today, education, the classroom, is a battleground. There are debates about the canon and what books are being taught and what topics. There are charges that campuses are run by leftists, by Marxist professors. David Horowitz is prominent among those who promote these kinds of ideas. From your perspective over the years, is this issue more acute now or does it ebb and flow?

There has always been a conflict in the educational world. There has always been scrutiny of what young people learn, scrutiny of their textbooks, scrutiny of their teachers. And for a simple reason—that education has always been dangerous to the establishment, and therefore the risk that is taken when young people go into the classroom is a risk that the people in charge of the status quo want to watch very carefully. I remember that back in the 1950s, during the McCarthy period, Harold Velde, the congressman from Illinois, got up to talk about a proposal in Congress to fund mobile library units to go into rural areas with trucks of books because the people in rural areas did not have access to libraries. And Velde got up and opposed this idea of mobile libraries because, he said,

"Education is the first step toward communism." While I don't think it's quite literally true, I think it is true that education has dangerous possibilities, always has had, and therefore it is guarded very, very carefully and attempts to control it have always existed.

The question is, what is going on now, is this a more intense attempt to control the education of young people than we have had in the past? And I think that may be so, for one reason. And that is, the stakes today for the United States are higher than they ever were before. That is, with the United States the predominant power in the world and seeking to establish its power, assert its power, consolidate its power, extend its power into more areas of the world, there is an enormous amount at stake for the establishment in bringing up a generation of young people who will accept what the United States government does, who will not be critical of it. In such a situation, where so much is at stake, where an empire is at stake, then it becomes more important to make sure that young people are not becoming critical of this empire, that we're not producing a young generation of skeptics and activists. And I think that may account for the special intensity today of the search for Marxists or leftists in the educational system.

The Canadian-born economist John Kenneth Galbraith once said that the paradox of the United States was "private wealth and public squalor." Here is a story on page 16 in the New York Times. *In Steinbeck's hometown of Salinas, California, where they're facing record deficits, the town is closing the three public libraries, including those named for Steinbeck and one for Cesar Chavez. Salinas is a town of one hundred fifty thousand largely composed of poor farm workers and immigrants. And the article goes on to say that this is part of a larger pattern. Libraries around the country are encountering hard times. Libraries in forty-one states absorbed more than fifty million dollars in financing cuts in the last year, and that more than eleven hundred libraries have reduced operating hours or trimmed their staffs. Jan Neal, the administrative manager of the Steinbeck branch that's slated to close, said, "Operating a library isn't as simple as selling cans of tomato soup at a retail store."*

It's interesting that that item appeared on page 16 of the *New York Times*. It should have appeared on page 1, because if it did, it might alert more people to what is really a horrifying development today. And that is, with huge sums of money going to war, with the military budget presented by Bush just calling for over four hundred billion dollars, plus another eighty billion dollars to pay for wars in Afghanistan and Iraq, in this kind of situation, there is no money for libraries, no money for schools, no money for arts programs in schools, no money for medical care, for hospitals, for health centers, for legal aid for the poor, for scholarships for students. What is happening to these libraries is symptomatic of something larger in the society, and that is the depletion of the wealth of this country for purposes of war and the starving of human resources in education and health. What is happening in Salinas, California, should be a wake-up call. Unfortunately, I would guess that this item has not been broadcast on national television and has not appeared, probably, in most newspapers around the country. It appears on page 16 of the *New York Times*, but it is something that is so far going unnoticed.

To me, it would be a very important thing to bring this to the attention of a larger public because I think it does have an immediate resonance with most people. I think most people do not like to see libraries closed. Most people would like to see their kids go to libraries and have books available to them. And I think if this were made a national issue and this very stark question would be posed to people, "Would you rather have your tax money go for libraries or would you rather have your tax money go for war?" I think the result of that would be an overwhelming one in favor of the libraries. But it's an example of the concealing—page 16—of information that might excite the population to action.

And it doesn't get the kind of attention that, say, the break-up of Hollywood stars like Brad Pitt and Jennifer Aniston does.

Let me just interject a personal note about libraries. As a kid growing up in a roach-infested tenement on the Upper East Side, the public library—I remember it very well, the Webster branch on Seventy-eighth Street and York Avenue was a refuge for me. There were no books at home. The library was a place that I could get away from the roaches and also find books.

But this attack on libraries, on schools, is it part of a pattern of undermining the commons?

Let me interject my own personal note, because it seems that you and I both grew up in cockroach-infested tenements but in different parts of New York, and we both had the same experience, that there were no books in my house. And so I would go to a library in East New York on the corner of Stone and Sutter. I still remember that library. And that was my refuge, just as you had your refuge. And it was a wonderful eye-opener for me and mind-opener for me.

But your question is a larger one. And that is, what is happening to the public commons? That is what Galbraith pointed to back when he wrote *The Affluent Society*. What has been really one of the terrible consequences of the militarization of the country is the starving of the public sector, the starving of education, of libraries, of health, of housing, and instead, of course, the pouring of money into activities that are enormously profitable for corporations.

This is why people become socialists. People become socialists in the way that I became a socialist when I read Upton Sinclair, and when I read Karl Marx, just to make it a little more dangerous. And that is the understanding that when you have a society where the production of things is based on their profitability, then the things that are not profitable will not be produced. And it is profitable to build high-rise luxury apartments. It is profitable to build banks and insurance companies, skyscrapers, as we have here in Boston. The tallest buildings are not residential buildings for poor people; they are John Hancock and Prudential. It is profitable to do those things, but it's not profitable to build housing for poor people. It is profitable to build nuclear weapons, profitable to build aircraft carriers and submarines. It is not profitable to build libraries or to build health care centers.

I talked about the militarization of society. But even before the United States began to turn an enormous amount of its wealth over to war, the very fact that we were a capitalist society based upon the profit motive meant that profit came first. After all, when Roosevelt confronted the depression, when the nation was in economic chaos, the nation had not yet become a militarized nation, but the nation had been a capitalist country. And in a capitalist country, the needs of people came second to the needs of big business. So this has been a constant factor in the United States as a capitalist society, only exacerbated by the militarization of the country.

Without overstating what ancient Athens was, let's say it was some kind of functioning democracy. It was always juxtaposed with Sparta, a highly militarized, aggressive, bellicose state. Is the United States drifting closer to Sparta?

Drifting may be an understatement. I think we're moving closer and closer to a controlled society. But it may be that the United States will be more like Athens than like Sparta, more like Athens in the sense that Athens had a kind of semblance of democracy, it had a veneer of democracy, but essentially Athens was controlled by an elite who maintained a slave society and who went to war for empire. In that sense, the United States resembles Athens more than Sparta. But it also, you might say, like Athens, became more like Sparta. As wars became more frequent, as the society became more militarized here in the United States we have become closer to the control of ideas and information, control of people's movements, the detention of people without trial, the destruction of the Bill of Rights, just as Athens, when it embarked on the Peloponnesian War against Sparta, became a less free society and a more cruel society. And I think in that sense the United States is playing the same kind of role.

You mentioned Karl Marx and the influence he had on you. There are lots of distortions and misrepresentations attached to Marx. His name, Marxist and Marxism, has became terms of derision and deprecation. Should people be reading Marx today?

Yes. But I wouldn't advise them to immediately plunge into Volume II or III of *Das Kapital*, maybe not even Volume I, which is formidable. But I think *The Communist Manifesto*, although the title may scare people, is still very much worth reading because what it does is to suggest to people who will read it that the capitalist society we have today is not eternal. *The Communist Manifesto* presents a historical view of the world in which we live. It shows you that societies have evolved from one form to another, one social system to another, from very primitive communal societies to feudal societies to capitalist societies. That capitalist society has come into being only in the last few hundreds years, and that happened as a result of the inadequacy of feudal society, the failure of feudal society to deal with the change in technology that was sort of inexorably happening, the commercialization, industrialization, new tools and implements. Capitalist society was able to deal with this new technology and to enhance it enormously.

But what Marx pointed out—and I think this is a very important insight—is that capitalist society, while it's developed the economy in an enormously impressive way, increased geometrically the number of goods available, nevertheless did not distribute the results of this enormous production equitably, the result being a small rich class and a large class of people who did not benefit from this enormous production. So Marx pointed to a fundamental flaw in capitalism, a flaw that should be evident to people today, especially in the United States. Here is this enormously productive and advanced technological country, and yet more than forty-five million people are without health insurance, one out of five children grow up in poverty, and millions of people are homeless and hungry.

What Marx does is to look at this fact, that almost anybody who looks at the United States today can see, and to put it in a historical context, and to say, The system that produced this came into being. It does not always have to exist. There could be another way of producing and distributing goods in society that would be more equitable, more human, where human needs would come first. And I think that insight, reading Marx, would be important to people.

I think another thing that would be important is Marx's class analysis, that is, Marx's view that when you look beneath the surface of political conflicts or cultural conflicts, you find class conflict. That the important question to ask in any situation is, who benefits from this, what class benefits from this? If Americans understood this Marxian concept of class, then, when they went to the polls and they had to choose between the Republican and Democratic party, they would ask, Which class does this party represent? When they study legislation put up before Congress, and the Bush administration proposed a certain tax program, people would ask, Which class does this tax program benefit? They wouldn't simply be doing what the newspapers do, which is to put the whole issue in terms of generalities, tax cut or tax increase, with no indication of which class will be hurt by this tax cut, which class will benefit by this rise in taxes. So a class analysis that people find in reading Marx, I think would be very useful in understanding American society today.

There was a peace march in Taos, New Mexico, on February 15, 2003. The lead banner read NO FLAG IS LARGE ENOUGH TO COVER THE SHAME OF KILLING INNOCENT PEOPLE. *That's a quote from you. How is patriotism being used today?*

Patriotism is being used today the way patriotism has always been used, and that is to try to encircle everybody in the nation into a common cause, the cause being the support of war and the advance of national power. Patriotism is used to create the illusion of a common interest that everybody in the country has. I just mentioned the necessity to see society in class terms, to realize that we do not have a common interest in our society, that people have different interests. What patriotism does is to pretend to a common interest. And the flag is the symbol of that common interest. So patriotism plays the same role that certain phrases in our national language play, and that is to create the illusion of common interest. The words that are used are *national security*, pretending that there is only one security for everybody, one kind of security for everybody; *national interest*, pretending that there is one interest for everybody; *national defense*, pretending that the word *defense* applies equally to all of us. So patriotism is a way of mobilizing people for causes that may not be in the people's interest.

It was Mark Twain, if I could paraphrase him, who said—at a point of another surge in U.S. imperialism, around 1900—that he supports the country all the time and the government when it earns it.

That I think is a very important distinction that Mark Twain captured in that statement, the distinction between country and government. You will hear young people who are marching off to war being interrogated by television reporters and asked, "Why are you going to Iraq?" or wherever they are being sent to at the time, and the young person will say, "I'm going to fight for my country." That requires a very close examination. Is this young person going to fight for his or her country, or is that person going to fight for the government?

It is the government that has decided on war; it is not the country. It is not the people who decide on war. There is a small group of people in Washington who decided on war and who are now trying to get everybody in the country to support this war by saying this war is for the benefit of the country. But, no, the country is not the government.

This is a point made by the Declaration of Independence, the fundamental philosophical statement of democracy in our history—

that governments are artificial creations, set up by the people, to support the equal right of people to life, liberty, and the pursuit of happiness, and when governments become destructive of those purposes and those ends, it is the right of the people to alter or abolish the government. Those are the words of the Declaration of Independence. So the Declaration of Independence makes that distinction. Governments are artificial entities. They are not the country. The country is the people.

So Twain's distinction is enormously important for people to understand if they are not to be swept up in what Kurt Vonnegut called a *granfalloon*, this great abstraction that envelops people into an artificial unity.

The United States is the only country in history to use weapons of mass destruction. The year 2005 marks the sixtieth anniversary of the bombings of Hiroshima and Nagasaki. That anniversary, incidentally, comes amid reports that the United States is developing a new generation of nuclear weapons. Where were you when the bombs were dropped, and do you remember your thoughts at the time?

I remember very clearly because I had just returned with my air force crew from Europe. We had been flying bombing missions in Europe, and the war in Europe was over, but the war in Asia with Japan was still on. And we flew back to this country in late July of 1945. We were all given a thirty-day furlough before reporting back for duty, with the intention that we would then go over to the Pacific and continue in the air war against Japan.

I had been married just before going overseas, and my wife and I decided on this thirty-day furlough that we would go off into the country for a little vacation. We were there waiting at the bus stop to take us into the country, and there was this newsstand and the big headline, ATOMIC BOMB DROPPED ON HIROSHIMA. Because the headline was so big, although I didn't know what an atomic bomb was, I assumed it must be a huge bomb. And my immediate reaction was, Well, maybe then I won't have to go to Japan. Maybe this means the end of the war on Japan. So I was happy; my wife was happy.

I must say, it was not until I was discharged from the army, the war was over, not until then did I think back to the bombing of Hiroshima. It was not until then that I began to question the bombing of Hiroshima. And that questioning began when I read John Hersey's book, *Hiroshima*, which is based on a series of articles he wrote for *The New Yorker*. He had gone to Hiroshima after the bombing and spoken to survivors. You can imagine what the survivors looked like—people without arms, legs, blinded, their skin something that you couldn't bear to look at. John Hersey spoke to these survivors of Hiroshima and wrote down their stories. When I read that, for the first time the effects of bombing on human beings came to me.

Here I had dropped bombs in Europe, but I had not seen anybody on the ground because when you're bombing from thirty thousand feet, you don't see anybody, you don't hear screams, you don't see blood; you don't know what's happening to human beings. You don't see kids with mangled limbs. And so I really had no idea of what the human consequences of my bombs were. Of course, this tells me today how easy it is for American pilots to fly over Iraq or any other place and drop bombs and not really know what they are doing to human beings.

So when I read John Hersey, it came to me what bombing did to human beings. We talked before about a book changing your life. That book changed my idea not just about bombing, but it profoundly changed my view of war because it made me realize that war now, in our time, in the time of high-level bombing and long-range shelling and death at a distance, inevitably means the indiscriminate killing of huge numbers of people, and therefore cannot be accepted as a way of solving problems.

The fact is that American nuclear armament has proceeded since the end of World War II with the acquiescence of all the major cultural institutions, in fact, with the cooperation of educational institutions, which participated in the scientific development of so many of these newer weapons. But certainly the press—television, radio, newspapers—have always gone along with this, have not criticized this, even though it has been so obvious to anybody who looked at the situation more than five minutes that the United States was arming itself far, far beyond any possible need to defend this country against attack. And so I'm not really surprised that this news of development of new nuclear weapons is going without criticism.

Of course, the real problem will be how will the American people respond, and how can an antiwar movement respond to this. How can an antiwar movement, which is concentrated right now on the war in Iraq, realize that quietly behind the scenes, the United States is increasing its nuclear capacity?

How do you make the case for being radical today?

We are faced today with a ruthless administration and with a Democratic Party that is cowardly in its failure to be a true opposition party. And the path we are on is more dangerous than any in a long time, a war without end, a theft of the national treasury to pay for war, a determination to ignore all international law and take whatever military action the president decides on. We therefore need, more than ever, a bold movement for radical departure from the present policies. Unless you offer solutions, people will turn away. Because if there is nothing you can do about a problem, what's the point of thinking about it?

While you often talk about Iraq, you don't usually mention Israel. Why not?

It's true, I don't deliberately bring up Israel often enough. But when I talk about terrorism, I explain that the only solution for terrorism is to get at the root of it, and that the root in the case of September 11 is U.S. foreign policy. And I point out that the elements of U.S. foreign policy most infuriating to people in the Middle East, and to the people who have carried out terrorist attacks, were the sanctions on Iraq, the stationing of U.S. troops in Saudi Arabia and elsewhere in the Middle East, and U.S. support for the Israeli occupation. I undoubtedly should pay more attention to the issue of Israel because of all the provocations, that is the greatest, and it is the one thought about most often throughout the Arab world.

Have there been comparable periods in U.S. history when Christian fundamentalists have been as visible and influential as they are today?

There have always been Christian fundamentalists who represented the most reactionary elements of American society, from the Salem witch hunts on. But never have they been such an important force in national policy, never so openly embraced by the president.

What can someone with your politics say to a Christian fundamentalist? The Bible does not have one message but many, and it is up to us as human beings to choose the message we think is most compassionate to others. If we want to retain our individual freedom, we must not simply obey some religious leader who will interpret the Bible for us. If we are thinking beings, we have a right to read and interpret for ourselves.

You've said it doesn't matter that much who's in the White House as much as who's outside in the streets. Do you still feel that way?

My statement is about the relative importance of both. Yes, it is important who sits in the White House, especially at certain critical moments in our history, when even a small difference between the political parties may be the difference between war and peace. But it is even more important to have a citizenry aroused, organized, mobilized, speaking up, putting pressure on whoever is in the White House. It is not clear if someone else in the White House today would be waging this war, but it is clear to me that if we had an antiwar movement strong enough, widespread enough, threatening enough to the people in power, even the war hawks now in the White House would have to reconsider their policy.

How is organizing today different than it was the 1960s?

Power is more tightly concentrated at the top, in politics, in the corporate world, in the media. The establishment learned from the 1960s to fight a war with minimum casualties on our side, to control information more closely, to lie more brazenly, to use the media more effectively to broadcast those lies. Those are real obstacles we have to confront.

What are the fissures in power that can be opened wider?

The growing disaffection—of soldiers and soldiers' families—from the war constitutes an area of real danger for this administration.

That's why, for instance, parents opposing military recruitment of their children in high school is so important.

Talk about Social Security: Why are efforts being made to privatize it coming now?

The Social Security system is only in danger if policies are put into effect that will endanger it—like privatization. The Social Security fund can be made adequate by applying the tax in a progressive way to the wealthiest part of the population, who now have a cap on what they contribute to the fund. Clearly, the economic interests behind Bush see in privatization great opportunities for profit. I think it also should be seen as part of a general push to do away with government support of social programs like Medicare and Medicaid.

What's the possibility of reviving the union movement? What needs to be done to make that happen?

I think two factors are involved in reviving the union movement. One is the state of the economy, which may push more and more people who are unorganized to form unions in self-protection. The other factor is a deliberate effort on the part of the trade union movement to organize the unorganized, who are now mostly in the service field, to undertake the kind of militant, aggressive organizing that was done by the CIO in the 1930s.

In 1963 you were fired from your job at Spelman College. In 2005 you returned to Spelman. Describe what happened.

I was fired from Spelman College by the college's first black president, a conservative man under pressure from a conservative board of trustees to get rid of troublemakers. It would not have looked good to fire me when I was with the students in their anti-segregation sit-ins and demonstrations. But when the Spelman students returned from jail, fired up, determined now to protest against their treatment on campus, the paternalism, the restrictions, and I supported them, that was too much for the president. He gave no reason for firing me in the letter informing me that my job was finished. I was a full professor with tenure, chair of the department. But when other people asked for the reason, he told it them it was "insubordination." Quite true.

Spelman has changed. The legacy of 1960s' activism is remembered. There is a new president, a progressive young woman, who undoubtedly played a key role in having the faculty and trustees vote to invite me back for an honorary degree and to give the commencement address in 2005. [See Afterword.]

You're sometimes described as an anarchist or a democratic socialist. Are you comfortable with those terms? What do they mean to you?

How comfortable I am with those terms depends on who's using them. I'm not uncomfortable when you use them. But if somebody is using them whom I suspect does not really know what those terms mean, then I feel uncomfortable because I feel they need clarification because, after all, the term *anarchist* to so many people means somebody who throws bombs, somebody who commits terrorist acts, somebody who believes in violence. Oddly enough, the term *anarchist* does not apply to governments, which use bombs on an enormous scale. The term *anarchist* has always applied to individuals who have used violence. So the term *anarchism* very often means that to people. Since I do not believe in throwing bombs, in terrorism or violence, I don't want that definition of anarchism to apply to me.

Anarchism is also misrepresented as being a society in which there is no organization, there is no responsibility, that there is a kind of chaos, again not realizing the irony of a world that is very chaotic, a society that is very chaotic, but to which the word *anarchism* is not applied.

I've only really, since the 1960s, begun to learn something about anarchism, in reading the autobiography of Emma Goldman, reading Alexander Berkman, Peter Kropotkin, and Michael Bakunin. Anarchism means to me a society in which you have a democratic organization of society, of decision making, of the economy; in which the authority of the capitalist is no longer there—the authority of the police and the courts and all the instruments of control that we have in modern society do not operate to control the actions of people. The people would have a say in their own destinies, in which they're not forced to choose between two political parties, neither of which represents their interests. So I see anarchism as meaning both political and economic democracy in the best sense of the term.

I see socialism, which is another term that I would accept comfortably, as meaning not the police state of the Soviet Union. After all, the word *socialism* has been commandeered by too many people, who, in my opinion, are not socialists but totalitarians. To me, socialism means a society that is egalitarian and in which the economy is geared to human needs instead of to business profits.

The theme of the World Social Forum is "Another World Is Possible." If you were to close your eyes for a moment, what kind of world might you envision?

The world that I envision—and I'm sure it will come to pass in a few weeks—is a world, first of all, that you might say was represented by the one hundred thousand people came together in the World Social Forum in Pôrto Alegre, Brazil. By that I mean, these are people who came from all over the world and who discarded their nationalist pride and nationalist hostility when they came together and tried to create a solidarity among people all over the world. So the world that I envision is one in which national boundaries no longer exist, in which you can move from one country to another with the same ease in which we can move from Massachusetts to Connecticut today, a world without passports or visas or immigration quotas. True globalization in the human sense, in which we recognize that the world is one and that human beings everywhere have the same rights.

In a world like that, you could not make war because it is your family, just as we here in this state are not thinking of making war on an adjoining state or even a far-off state. No, war comes from the creation of interests that are national interests and that see people who live across another border as enemies. A world without borders could not have enemies that you could make war on.

It would be a world in which the riches of the planet would be distributed in an equitable fashion, where we wouldn't have the kind of situation we have today of rich countries and poor countries—of industrialized countries where everybody at least has access to clean water vis à vis the rest of the world where a billion people have no access to clean water. Yes, that would take some organization to make sure that the riches of the earth are distributed according to human need.

And a world in which people are free to speak, a world in which there was a true bill of rights. A world in which people were freer to express themselves because political rights and free speech rights are really dependent on economic status and having fundamental economic needs taken care of.

Yes, I think it would be a world in which the boundaries of race and religion and nation would not become causes for antagonism. Even though there would still be cultural differences and still be language differences, there would not be causes for violent action of one against the other.

I think it would be a world in which people would not have to work more than a few hours a day, which is possible with our technology. It's possible with the technology available today. If this technology were not used in the way it is now used, for war and for wasteful activities, people could work three or four hours a day and produce enough to take care of any needs. So it would be a world in which people had more time for music and sports and literature and just living in a human way with others.

You've said that you got into history for a very modest reason: "I wanted to change the world." How close have you come to reaching your goal?

As I said, I'm just a few weeks away. All I can say is, I hope that by my writing and by my speaking, whatever I've done, by my activity, that I have moved at least a few people toward a greater understanding and moved at least a few people toward becoming more active citizens. And so I feel that my contribution, along with the contribution of millions of other people, if they continue, and if they are passed on to more and more people and if our numbers grow, yes, one day—I won't give a date—we may very well see the kind of world that I envision.

AFTERWORD

"AGAINST DISCOURAGEMENT"

In 1963 Howard Zinn was fired from Spelman College, where he was chair of the history department, for "insubordination." He had supported his students with whom he had been active in the movement against racial segregation, and who then rebelled against a paternalistic college administration. In May of 2005, he was invited back by Spelman to receive an honorary degree and to give the commencement address. Here is the text of that speech.

I am deeply honored to be invited back to Spelman after forty-two years. I would like to thank the faculty and trustees who voted to invite me, and especially your president, Dr. Beverly Tatum. And it is a special privilege to be here with Diahann Carroll and Virginia Davis Floyd.

But this is your day—the students graduating today. It's a happy day for you and your families. I know you have your own hopes for the future, so it may be a little presumptuous for me to tell you what hopes I have for you, but they are exactly the same ones that I have for my grandchildren.

My first hope is that you will not be too discouraged by the way the world looks at this moment. It is easy to be discouraged because our nation is at war—still another war, war after war—and our government seems determined to expand its empire even if it costs the lives of tens of thousands of human beings. There is poverty in this country, and homelessness, and people without health care, and crowded classrooms, but our government, which has trillions of dollars to spend, is spending its wealth on war. There are a billion people in Africa, Asia, Latin America, and the Middle East who need clean water and medicine to deal with malaria and tuberculosis and AIDS, but our government, which has thousands of nuclear weapons, is experimenting with even more deadly nuclear weapons. Yes, it is easy to be discouraged by all that.

But let me tell you why, in spite of what I have just described, you must not be discouraged.

I want to remind you that fifty years ago racial segregation here in the South was entrenched as tightly as was apartheid in South Africa. The national government, even with liberal presidents like Kennedy and Johnson in office, was looking the other way while black people were beaten and killed and denied the opportunity to vote. So black people in the South decided they had to do something by themselves. They boycotted and sat in and picketed and demonstrated, and were beaten and jailed, and some were killed, but their cries for freedom were soon heard all over the nation and around the world, and the president and Congress finally did what they had previously failed to do—enforce the Fourteenth and Fifteenth Amendments to the Constitution. Many people had said: The South will never change. But it did change. It changed because ordinary people organized and took risks and challenged the system and would not give up. That's when democracy came alive.

I want to remind you also that when the war in Vietnam was going on, and young Americans were dying and coming home paralyzed, and our government was bombing the villages of Vietnam—bombing schools and hospitals and killing ordinary people in huge numbers—it looked hopeless to try to stop the war. But just as in the southern movement, people began to protest and soon it caught on. It was a national movement. Soldiers were coming back and denouncing the war, and young people were refusing to join the military, and the war had to end.

The lesson of that history is that you must not despair, that if you are right, and you persist, things will change. The government may try to deceive the people, and the newspapers and television may do the same, but the truth has a way of coming out. The truth has a power greater than a hundred lies. I know you have practical things to do—to get jobs and get married and have children. You may become prosperous and be considered a success in the way our society defines success, by wealth and standing and prestige. But that is not enough for a good life.

Remember Tolstoy's story, *The Death of Ivan Illych*. A man on his deathbed reflects on his life, how he has done everything right, obeyed the rules, become a judge, married, had children, and is looked upon as a success. Yet in his last hours he wonders why he feels a failure. After becoming a famous novelist, Tolstoy himself had decided that this was not enough, that he must speak out against the treatment of the Russian peasants, that he must write against war and militarism.

My hope is that whatever you do to make a good life for yourself—whether you become a teacher, or social worker, or business person, or lawyer, or poet, or scientist—you will devote part of your life to making this a better world for your children, for all children. My hope is that your generation will demand an end to war, that your generation will do something that has not yet been done in history and wipe out the national boundaries that separate us from other human beings on this earth.

Recently I saw a photo on the front page of the *New York Times*, which I cannot get out of my mind. It showed ordinary Americans sitting on chairs on the southern border of Arizona, facing Mexico. They were holding guns and they were looking for Mexicans who might be trying to cross the border into the United States. This was horrifying to me—the realization that in this twenty-first century of what we call civilization we have carved up what we claim is one world into two hundred artificially created entities we call "nations" and are ready to kill anyone who crosses a boundary.

Is not nationalism—that devotion to a flag, an anthem, a boundary so fierce it leads to murder—one of the great evils of our time, along with racism, along with religious hatred? These ways of thinking, cultivated, nurtured, indoctrinated from childhood on, have been useful to those in power, deadly for those out of power.

Here in the United States, we are brought up to believe that our nation is different from others, an exception in the world, uniquely moral; that we expand into other lands in order to bring civilization, liberty, democracy. But if you know some history, you know that's not true. If you know some history, you know we massacred Indians on this continent, invaded Mexico, sent armies into Cuba and the Philippines. We killed huge numbers of people, and we did not bring them democracy or liberty. We did not go into Vietnam to bring democracy; we did not invade Panama to stop the drug trade; we did not invade Afghanistan and Iraq to stop terrorism. Our aims were the aims of all the other empires of world history—more profit for corporations, more power for politicians.

The poets and artists among us seem to have a clearer understanding of the disease of nationalism. Perhaps the black writers especially are less enthralled with the virtues of American "liberty" and "democracy," their people having enjoyed so little of it. I am speaking of Langston Hughes, Zora Neale Hurston, Richard Wright, and James Baldwin.

I am a veteran of the Second World War. That was considered a "good war," but I have come to the conclusion that war solves no fundamental problems and leads only to more wars. War poisons the minds of soldiers, leads them to kill and torture, and poisons the soul of the nation.

My hope is that your generation will demand that your children be brought up in a world without war. It we want a world in which the people of all countries are brothers and sisters, if the children all over the world are considered as our children, then war—in which children are always the greatest casualties—cannot be accepted as a way of solving problems.

I was on the faculty of Spelman College for seven years, from 1956 to 1963. It was a heartwarming time because the friends we made in those years have remained our friends all these years. My wife, Roslyn, and I and our two children lived on campus. Sometimes when we went into town, white people would ask: How is it to be living in the black community? It was hard to explain. But we knew this—that in downtown Atlanta, we felt as if we were in alien territory, and when we came back to the Spelman campus, we felt that we were at home.

Those years at Spelman were the most exciting of my life, the most educational certainly. I learned more from my students than they learned from me. Those were the years of the great movement in the South against racial segregation, and I became involved in that in Atlanta; in Albany, Georgia; in Selma, Alabama; in Hattiesburg, Mississippi; and Greenwood and Itta Bena and Jackson. I learned something about democracy: that it does not come from the government, from on high, it comes from people getting together and struggling for justice. I learned about race. I learned something that any intelligent person realizes at a certain point— that race is a manufactured thing, an artificial thing, and while race does matter (as Cornel West has written), it matters only because certain people want it to matter, just as nationalism is something artificial. I learned that what really matters is that all of us—of whatever so-called race and so-called nationality—are human beings and should cherish one another.

I was lucky to be at Spelman at a time when I could watch a marvelous transformation in my students, who were so polite, so quiet, and then suddenly they were leaving the campus and going into town, and sitting in, and being arrested, and then coming out of jail full of fire and rebellion. You can read all about that in Harry Lefever's book *Undaunted by the Fight*. One day Marian Wright (now Marian Wright Edelman), who was my student at Spelman, and was one of the first arrested in the Atlanta sit-ins, came to our house on campus to show us a petition she was about to put on the bulletin board of her dormitory. The heading on the petition epitomized the transformation taking place at Spelman College. Marian had written on top of the petition YOUNG LADIES WHO CAN PICKET, PLEASE SIGN BELOW.

My hope is that you will not be content just to be successful in the way that our society measures success; that you will not obey the rules when the rules are unjust; that you will act out the courage that I know is in you. There are wonderful people, black and white, who are models. I don't mean African Americans like Condoleezza Rice, or Colin Powell, or Clarence Thomas, who have become servants of the rich and powerful. I mean W. E. B. DuBois and Martin Luther King and Malcolm X and Marian Wright Edelman, and James Baldwin and Josephine Baker and good white folk, too, who defied the establishment to work for peace and justice.

Another of my students at Spelman, Alice Walker, who, like Marian, has remained our friend all these years, came from a tenant farmer's family in Eatonton, Georgia, and became a famous writer. In one of her first published poems, she wrote:

It is true—
I've always loved
the daring
*   ones*
Like the black young
man
Who tried
to crash
All barriers
at once,
*   wanted to*
swim
At a white
beach (in Alabama)
Nude.

I am not suggesting you go that far, but you can help to break down barriers, of race certainly but also of nationalism; that you do what you can—you don't have to do something heroic, just something, to join with millions of others who will just do something because all of those somethings, at certain points in history, come together and make the world better.

That marvelous African American writer Zora Neale Hurston, who wouldn't do what white people wanted her to do, who wouldn't do what black people wanted her to do, who insisted on being herself, said that her mother advised her: Leap for the sun—you may not reach it, but at least you will get off the ground.

By being here today, you are already standing on your toes, ready to leap. My hope for you is a good life.

—Howard Zinn

ACKNOWLEDGMENTS

Special thanks to:

Anthony Arnove, peerless editor and dear friend, Elaine Bernard of the Harvard Trade Union Program for her extraordinary solidarity and providing space for four of the interviews; Greg Gigg for his good cheer and car rides, HarperCollins editors Hugh Van Dusen and Marie Estrada for their enthusiasm for the book and shepherding it through; KGNU community radio in Boulder and Denver, where two of the interviews were recorded; the Lannan Foundation in Santa Fe, New Mexico; and Martin Voelker for his esprit de corps and techinal support.

Most of all, thanks to Howard Zinn. He has long been a mainstay of Alternative Radio. This is our second book together (following *The Future History*). The questions were unrehearsed. We've tried to keep the conversational tone, spontaneity, and humor. Working with him is a privilege and joy. And yes, he's an original.

David Barsamian
Boulder, Colorado
February 6, 2006

ABOUT *ALTERNATIVE RADIO*

Alternative Radio (http://www.alternativeradio.org/) is a weekly one-hour public affairs program offered free to all public radio stations in the United States, Canada, Europe, South Africa, Australia, and on short-wave on Radio for Peace International. AR provides information, analyses, and views that are frequently ignored or distorted in other media.

Established in 1986 in Boulder, Colorado, AR is dedicated to the founding principles of public broadcasting, which urge that programming serve as "a forum for controversy and debate," be diverse, and "provide a voice for groups that may otherwise be unheard." The project is entirely independent, sustained solely by individuals who buy transcripts and CDs of programs. AR reaches more than one hundred twenty-five radio stations and millions of listeners. It is part of the nonprofit Institute for Social and Cultural Change.

BOOKS BY
HOWARD ZINN

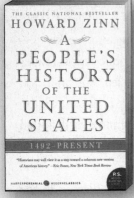

A PEOPLE'S HISTORY OF THE UNITED STATES

1492–Present

ISBN 0-06-052837-0 (paperback)
ISBN 0-694-52203-1 (cassette)
ISBN 0-06-053006-5 (CD)

Newly revised and updated from its original landmark publication in 1980. Zinn throws out the official version of history taught in schools—with emphasis on great men in high places—to focus on the street, the home, and the workplace. This latest edition contains two new chapters that cover the Clinton presidency, the 2000 election, and the "War on Terrorism."

"Historians may well view it as a step toward a coherent new version of American history."
—Eric Foner, *New York Times Book Review*

PASSIONATE DECLARATIONS
Essays on War and Justice
ISBN 0-06-055767-2 (paperback)

A collection of essays that focus on American political ideology. With a new preface by the author.

"A shotgun blast of revisionism that aims to shatter all the comfortable myths of American political discourse."
—*Los Angeles Times*

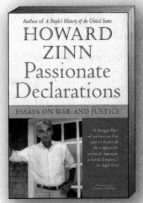

THE TWENTIETH CENTURY
A People's History

ISBN 0-06-053034-0 (paperback)

Designed for general readers and students of modern American history, this reissue of the twentieth-century chapters from Howard Zinn's popular *A People's History of the United States* is brought up-to-date with new chapters on Clinton's presidency, the 2000 election, and the "War on Terrorism."

"Professor Zinn writes with an enthusiasm rarely encountered in the leaden prose of academic history."
—*New York Times Book Review*

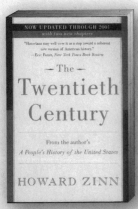

THE PEOPLE SPEAK
American Voices, Some Famous, Some Little Known

ISBN 0-06-057826-2 (paperback)
ISBN 0-06-058982-5 (cassette)
ISBN 0-06-058983-3 (CD)

A wonderful selection of American voices from Columbus to the present, interwoven with commentary by Zinn. Including selections from a Lowell Mill worker, Frederick Douglass, Mark Twain, Helen Keller, Malcolm X, and a Gulf War resister.

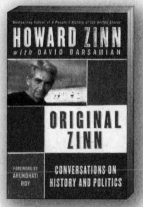

ORIGINAL ZINN
Conversations on History and Politics

ISBN 0-06-084425-6 (paperback)

For more than a decade, bestselling author and historian Howard Zinn has been interviewed by David Barsamian for Public Radio, and their wide-ranging conversations over the past five years are collected in *Original Zinn*. Subjects include: the Kennedy brothers; why sanctions are weapons of mass destruction; and the role of artists, like Langston Hughes and Bob Dylan, in relation to social change.